OLD TESTAMENT APOCALYPTIC

INTERPRETING BIBLICAL TEXTS

The Gospels, Fred B. Craddock
New Testament Apocalyptic, Paul S. Minear
The Pentateuch, Lloyd R. Bailey, Sr.
The Prophets, James M. Ward
Wisdom Literature and Psalms, Roland E. Murphy
Deuteronomic History, Terence E. Fretheim
The Pauline Letters,
Leander E. Keck and Victor Paul Furnish
Old Testament Apocalyptic, Paul D. Hanson

INTERPRETING  BIBLICAL TEXTS

Old Testament Apocalyptic

Paul D. Hanson

LLOYD R. BAILEY, SR.
and
VICTOR P. FURNISH, EDITORS

ABINGDON PRESS NASHVILLE

OLD TESTAMENT APOCALYPTIC

Second Printing 1988

Library of Congress Cataloging-in-Publication Data

HANSON, PAUL D.

Old Testament apocalyptic.

(Interpreting Biblical Texts)

1. Apocalyptic literature—History and criticism. 2. Bible. O.T. Isaiah—Criticism, interpretation, etc. 3. Bible. O.T. Zechariah—Criticism, interpretation, etc. 4. Bible. O.T. Daniel—Criticism, interpretation, etc. I. Title. II. Series.

BS646.H36 1987 221 87-11449

ISBN 0-687-28750-2 (soft: alk. paper)

Scripture quotations noted "author's trans." may also be found in Paul Hanson, *The Dawn of Apocalyptic* (Philadelphia: Fortress, 1975).

MANUFACTURED BY THE PARTHENON PRESS AT
NASHVILLE, TENNESSEE, UNITED STATES OF AMERICA

To

CARL E. KLEIMOLA

a
true friend
and constant
source of inspiration
on his
eighthieth birthday

INTERPRETING BIBLICAL TEXTS:
Editors' Foreword

The volumes in this series have been planned for those who are convinced that the Bible has meaning for our life today and who wish to enhance their skills as interpreters of the biblical texts. Such interpreters must necessarily engage themselves in two closely related tasks: (1) determining as much as possible about the original meaning of the various biblical writings, and (2) determining in what respect these texts are still meaningful today. The objective of the present series is to keep both of these tasks carefully in view and to provide assistance in relating the one to the other.

Because of this overall objective, it would be wrong to regard the individual volumes in this series as commentaries, as homiletical expositions of selected texts, or as abstract discussions of "the hermeneutical problem." Rather, they have been written in order to identify and illustrate what is involved in relating the meaning of the biblical texts in their own times to their meaning in ours. Biblical commentaries and other technical reference works sometimes focus exclusively on the first, paying little or no attention to the second. On the other hand, many attempts to expound the contemporary "relevance" of biblical themes or passages pay scant attention to the intentions of the texts themselves. And although one of the standard topics of "hermeneutics" is how a text's original meaning relates to its present meaning, such discussions often employ highly technical philosophical language and proceed with little reference to concrete examples. By way of contrast, the present volumes are written in language that will be understood by scholars, clergy, and laypersons alike, and they deal with concrete texts, actual problems of interpretation, and practical procedures for moving from "then" to "now."

Each contributor to this series is committed to three basic tasks: (1) a description of the salient features of the particular type of biblical literature or section of the canon assigned to him; (2) the identification and explanation of the basic assumptions that guide his analysis and explication of those materials; and (3) the discussion of possible contemporary meanings of representative texts, in view of the specified assumptions with which the interpreter approaches them.

The assumptions that are brought to biblical interpretation may vary from one author to the next and will undoubtedly differ from those of many readers. Nonetheless, we believe that the present series, by illustrating how careful interpreters carry out their tasks, will encourage readers to be more reflective about the way they interpret the Bible.

Lloyd R. Bailey, Sr.
Duke Divinity School

Victor P. Furnish
Perkins School of Theology
Southern Methodist University

CONTENTS

PART TWO—DO APOCALYPTIC TEXTS SPEAK TO OUR WORLD?

WHAT IS OLD TESTAMENT APOCALYPTIC?

PART ONE

I.
WHY STUDY THE APOCALYPTIC WRITINGS?

As people of faith, Jews and Christians look to the Bible as a trustworthy guide to a life that is both personally fulfilling and a source of blessing to others. Underlying this attitude is the conviction that "all scripture is inspired by God" and thus "profitable for teaching, for reproof, for correction, and for training in righteousness" (2 Tim 3:16). While such readers differ in the way they understand the divine inspiration of Scripture, the Bible occupies a unique role in influencing the ways in which they think about and respond to the issues of the world around them.

Given the wide span of history and the diversity of settings within which the biblical materials arose, it is quite surprising how unified is its essential message regarding the nature of the righteous life. God is to be placed at the very center of life, devotion to every idol is to be eschewed, and God's own outreach toward humans is to be our example, as we respond to God by means of lives dedicated to the well-being of others, regardless of gender, race, or class. In placing before us a vision of the harmonious order of righteousness and compassion intended by God for the human family, the witness of the Torah (Pentateuch), the Prophets, and the Gospels is united. And indeed, the *regula fidei* ("rule of faith") that developed over the course of the early history of the church presents clearly the character of the way of life that is faithful to God's initiating activity on behalf of humans.

The question of a biblically based faith is complicated somewhat by the presence of passages and even whole books about whose meaning and intent readers are confused. As a result, we may be inclined to dismiss such writings from our consideration, or to assign to them a lesser status that frees us from being open to their potential impact on our lives. The writings from the New Testament, which Paul Minear has addressed in a previous volume in this series,[1] and the Old Testament writings that provide the focus of the present volume are prime candidates for such indifferent or evasive treatment. Martin Luther and D. H. Lawrence may appear unlikely allies in the area of biblical interpretation, but their concurrence in questioning the value of the book of Revelation is indicative of the skepticism vis-à-vis the apocalyptic writings of the Bible.[2] Whether in the sixteenth century or the twentieth, whether among people within the church or outside, one need not look far to find reasons for many people's distaste for or even hostility to the words of the books of Daniel and Revelation or the smaller apocalyptic sections of Isaiah, Zechariah, Mark, and the Pauline Epistles. This is because they have at times been interpreted as a call to extreme actions, whether in the form of revolution, holy war against other nations, purging of dissidents within the church, or withdrawal from social and political involvement in anticipation of God's imminent intervention in history.

The problem raised by such applications of the apocalyptic writings has two sides. On the one, there emerges the difficult question of the meaning of these texts within their original social and historical settings. On the other, there emerges the problem of the proper application of apocalyptic texts to contemporary issues. Before one can feel motivated to examine these two sides of the problem, however, one must be open to the possibility that these writings are in fact of value to individuals and to communities of faith. While the case can finally be proven or disproven only in the actual interpretation of the texts themselves (to which we shall turn in Part 2), the following points are offered as preliminary indications that the apocalyptic writings must be taken seriously by contemporary believers.

1. Dread of the present and the future obviously

plagues many people in our day. If people of high moral principles do not address this sense of doom and pay attention to the various writings, songs, and films giving expression to it, people of lower moral principles will dominate the scene and drive our world ever closer to moral degeneracy and even to the abyss of nuclear catastrophe.

Let us consider one example of the misuse of an apocalyptic theme. On all levels of contemporary society, from the most humble of folk to those in the highest echelons of business and government, one is witnessing an increasingly popular system of interpretation, which uses the apocalyptic writings to defend the buildup and deployment of sophisticated weaponry, especially nuclear warheads, supposedly as a part of God's predetermined plan for judging the world.[3] According to this view, the dreadful day of judgment spoken of in Ezekiel 38–39, Isaiah 24, Zechariah 12, and Daniel 7–12 is imminent. The enemies of God's people (which these texts call Gog of Magog and the Beast) are typically identified with the Soviet Union, China, or world communism. Since, in the biblical materials, great trials must precede the final ecstasy of the chosen, a resultant modern longing for the end has fostered an attitude of belligerence toward the nations that have been identified with the forces of evil and has created a predisposition toward hostile confrontation with them as the means of hastening God's judgment upon the wicked and the salvation of the chosen.

It is not enough simply to dismiss this system of interpretation as inhumane or as a modern misunderstanding, for it reaches far back in the history of interpretation. It can be called into question only by an alternative understanding of these writings that is more compelling than its rivals. Above all, this would involve an approach that interprets the apocalyptic writings within the context of the theology of the entire Bible.

2. The second reason why we cannot avoid the apocalyptic theme is that it has become an irrepressible part of the contemporary consciousness. The optimism that once dismissed the grim imagery of apocalyptic, in view of steady progress toward prosperity, has been shattered by a far darker outlook. The words "apocalyptic" and "apocalypse" have been revived as everyday words in the vocabulary of politicians, military strategists, novelists, and religious leaders. In the progressive climate of the latter half of the nineteenth century and the ebullient Eisenhower era, projections of the future were based on empirical data gathered from production figures and growth charts. By contrast, commentators today seem to be preoccupied with less predictable, more arcane powers that seem to be impelling humanity inexorably closer to a catastrophe of unprecedented horror. Against this background, the struggle of apocalyptic seers with the

uncanny sides of life and with the influence of apparently superhuman forces on human destiny strikes a resonant chord, for we moderns stand face to face with powers that transcend human imagination in their awesome destructiveness. We, like Arjuna in the *Bhagavad Gita,* encounter a face of Krishna never before seen by humans, one as bright and terrible as "the radiance of a thousand suns" (11:12). We are forced to reckon with the possibility that our God, like Krishna, has declared: "I have become Death, the shatterer of worlds" (11:32).[4]

In this deeply ambivalent and troubled situation, one senses a growing openness to the apocalyptic writings. At the heart of the message of biblical apocalypticism is the belief that human experiences are not amenable to facile analysis. In the search for explanations of dimensions of reality that have baffled the consciousness of most humans, the apocalyptic writers often use symbols and narrative patterns that are as dark and impenetrable as the phenomena they seek to address. These symbols and patterns have tended to take on a new fascination for many people within the contemporary setting of confusion and dread vis-à-vis the future. It is the duty of the religious communities that continue to hand down the apocalyptic writings as a part of their heritage to guide such people to a proper understanding of these difficult and mysterious works and thereby to a life-enhancing approach to the troubling realities that afflict the modern consciousness.

3. A careful study of the apocalyptic writings exposes us to an analysis of human existence and an understanding of history that adds important dimensions of meaning to the theology of the Bible. Let us describe several of the important contributions made by these writings.

First, the apocalyptic visions are remarkably broad in their grasp of reality, as they carry further the universalistic tendencies that are already beginning to appear in the later prophets of Israel. They often survey history from primordial times to the eschaton. Spatially, their scope is cosmic, reaching from the heavens to the netherworld. This vast realm they seek to relate in its totality to the purposes of the one God who directs all nations and events according to a righteous plan. Though the biblical apocalyptic writings are filled with archaic and mythic idioms that require thorough translation, we find in them the rudiments of a view of history and an ontology that addresses the desire of many contemporary people to evolve a broadly inclusive world vision, one more capable of fostering peace than the barbaric nuclear tribalism that threatens us all.

Second, we find in the apocalyptic writings a courageous struggle with, and often a profound penetration into, the nature of the most troubling aspects of life. Among them are conflict between the nations, moral paradoxes, innocent suffering and martyrdom, and the failure of divine promises to come to fulfillment. It is a natural human tendency to deny that conflicts lie at the heart of life. But as Carl Jung explained:

> The sad truth is that man's real life consists of a complex of opposites—day and night, birth and death, happiness and misery, good and evil. We are not even sure that one will prevail against the other, that good will overcome evil, or joy defeat pain. Life is a battleground. It always has been, and always will be; and if it were not so, existence would come to an end.[5]

In an apparent unwillingness to settle for surface explanations, the apocalyptic writings seek to trace life's disruptive phenomena to their root causes, especially the pernicious forces of evil manifested by historical figures and mythical agents. Although modern readers may shy away from some of the mythological symbolism used in portraying both what disrupts and what restores the harmony intended by God, we stand to be instructed by the unflinching struggle with the question of theodicy that we find amid such symbolism, and by the unrelenting effort to trace to its source all the negativity that plagues life, so as to rediscover the divine order within which evil will be overcome.

Third, the apocalyptic writings continue to provide a trustworthy and durable basis for hope and courage to those who find that the trials of life have exhausted their human ability to cope. Before those in relatively untroubled circumstances dismiss the spiritual value of the apocalyptic sections of the Bible, they need to recall how precious the words of Daniel and Revelation have been to political prisoners, hunted dissidents, and those struggling daily to find sufficient food and water to sustain life, from ancient times down to this very day. One must remember the world experienced daily by Bishop Desmond Tutu of South Africa, village priests of Central America, and one's sisters and brothers in Ethiopia, in order to recognize the divine power present in the apocalyptic writings. It is a power that confronts the oppressed, preserves hope among the persecuted, strengthens the resolve of those confronting seemingly insurmountable obstacles, and gives assurance to those finally overcome by violence or starvation that God's love and power cannot be cut off from them even by death.

Fourth, the apocalyptic writings can nurture in us a sensitivity toward certain individuals and groups within our society whom others dismiss and belittle as deviant.[6] Not only can the presence of this kind of literature in the Bible remind us that the apocalyptic perception of life is legitimate, yes, perfectly normal under certain circumstances; it can also help us to accept the apocalyptic dimension of our own consciousness, that dimension which dares to peer deeply enough into the tensions and conflicts of our own lives and the world around us to recognize the magnitude of the struggle between good and evil that underlies them. Frequently, the grim symbolism of the apocalyptic mode more accurately describes the actual circumstances in which we live than is suggested by our sometimes facile optimism. The penetration of the apocalyptic vision to the root causes of the poverty, international tension, and injustice that we choose to ignore is far more likely to spur people of faith to action than is the narrow vision that allows the privileged of the earth to live under the illusion that their way of life is normal, justified, or even divinely ordained. Though the immediate effect of the apocalyptic vision may be a deep questioning of customary assumptions, attitudes, and actions, the end result may be transformations in knowledge, perspective, and commitment that equip faith communities to embody and promote the justice, mercy, and peace that God intends for all people.

II.
DEFINING OLD TESTAMENT APOCALYPTIC

A Working Definition

In any discussion, a term is only as useful as the clarity with which it is defined and the precision with which it is applied. Stated somewhat differently, a term is being used correctly to the extent that it promotes understanding of the matter being investigated. In the case of Old Testament apocalyptic, we are dealing with a term worthy of preservation only if it aids us in designating and understanding certain biblical writings that, while betraying connections with other types of literature, can best be studied as a discrete group.

Recent attempts to introduce precision into the definition and application of the term "apocalyptic" have proven difficult. Efforts to define it primarily by recourse to literary criteria have come up against the perplexing fact that limiting the apocalyptic corpus to writings that conform to a literary genre designated "apocalypse" excludes many writings that for other reasons seem to give expression to an apocalyptic view of reality. The attempt to define apocalyptic on the basis of its sources has also foundered. This has proved to be especially true of attempts to define apocalyptic as a development of the wisdom tradition, since this failed to account for the central role of eschatology in most apocalyptic writings. On the other hand, exclusive attention to biblical prophecy as the mother of apocalyptic, while explaining the centrality of eschatology, fails to explain certain speculative elements that occupy a conspicuous place in writings usually regarded as apocalyptic, among them observations relating to meteorological phenomena and astrological systems. Similarly, the description of apocalyptic as the use of ancient myth to express convictions about the end-time, while correctly drawing attention to the generous use of mythic motifs by many apocalyptic writers, is in itself too narrow an approach to account for many other facets of this literature.

The inadequacy of the above mentioned attempts to define Old Testament apocalyptic may seem to lead to the conclusion that a sociological definition would best serve our purposes, one that describes the type of social setting, or more specifically, the type of social group or movement that generates apocalyptic works, and then labels the works coming out of such groups or movements "apocalyptic." But problems also beset this approach. In most cases, it is very difficult to reconstruct the setting of an apocalyptic work. By nature, this type of literature offers few clues as to its historical and social home. What is more, apocalyptic elements are present in many works that stem from groups that cannot be designated strictly as apocalyptic movements, such as certain rabbinical circles.[1]

One element that has been left out of the above approaches to defining apocalyptic is the matter of the function of the writings in question. Apocalyptic writings foster hope in situations of crisis for those despairing of help from earthly sources. But this definition also proves inadequate by itself, even though it points to an important dimension in most apocalyptic writings, because other types of writing, such as psalms of supplication, also function in a similar manner.

In a book that aims at shedding light specifically on the apocalyptic writings of the Old Testament, it seems that a workable definition must combine aspects of several of the above definitions in such a way as to capture both what defines a certain group of writings as unique and what distinguishes such writings from others. Accordingly, one may define the Old Testament apocalyptic writings as follows:

A group of writings concerned with the renewal of faith and the reordering of life on the basis of a vision of a prototypical heavenly order revealed to a religious community through a seer. The author tends to relativize the significance of existing realities by depicting how they are about to be superseded by God's universal reign in an eschatological event that can neither be hastened nor thwarted by human efforts, but which will unfold, true to an eternal plan, as the result of divine action.

Let us consider in greater detail each part of this definition. The phrase "group of writings" is intentionally vague, since reference solely to those writings that conform to the literary type of the apocalypse would be too restrictive. As we shall indicate below, this in no way denies the importance of the specific genre of the apocalypse within the apocalyptic writings of the Old Testament.

The phrases "renewal of faith" and "reordering of life" point to two of the primary functions of the apocalyptic writings. They suggest a common background in which faith has been challenged and the normal structures of the community are either threatened or have collapsed. Two points often made in the scholarly literature are thus included within our definition: (1) Apocalyptic represents a crisis literature, and (2) apocalyptic writings are intended to offer comfort and hope to the afflicted. Two of the most common moods thus conveyed by these writings are consolation and exhortation.

At the heart of every apocalyptic writing is "a vision of a prototypical heavenly order." That is, they regard the heavenly world as the real world and as the source of the transformation awaited by the faithful. This central focus provides the point of entry for widely diverse mythological motifs and patterns, for mythological symbols offered to Jewish seers the ancient world's most familiar language for describing the supermundane. The focus on the transcendent realm was also the point at which many of the themes of ancient wisdom traditions could attach themselves, such as detailed descriptions of the heavenly and the divine order on its various levels. Eventually, this led to the literary device of a heavenly journey by the seer as a means of describing the revealed prototypical order.

The vision was "revealed to a religious community through a seer." Though great difficulties impede attempts to reconstruct the communities to which the apocalyptic writings were addressed, it is clear that we are dealing with a literature that was critical in the process by which certain groups within the larger Jewish community defined their identity. The clues contained in these writings suggest that we are often dealing with groups who were experiencing deprivation and alienation vis-à-vis the prevailing power structures. The apocalyptic vision gives expression to the social, political, and religious ideologies and beliefs of these groups in their struggles with antagonists either within the Jewish community or from foreign nations. Since this literature is typically anonymous or written under an assumed name, it is difficult to be more explicit about the mediator of the divine message than simply to refer to "the seer."

A vision "tending to relativize the significance of existing realities" is obviously a product of those experiencing the realities of this world as unsatisfying or even intolerable. When measured against the divine promises which such oppressed persons believed described their divinely intended destiny, this-worldly realities must have represented a sharp contradiction. Empowerment to cope with such negative realities comes through denying them any ultimate validity. Such denial assumes the form of a visionary depiction of events in heaven foreshadowing the end of the world as presently experienced, a world that is about to be "superseded by God's universal reign." All earthly powers, though inflicting much pain, are thus reduced to insignificance in an ultimate sense. This conviction of course turns the attention of seer and community to the future, to the vindication of the faithful by "an eschatological event that can neither be hastened nor thwarted by human efforts but which will unfold, true to an eternal plan, as the result of divine action." To lend credence to the apocalyptic vision of the future, the seer sometimes presents a résumé of past history (actually depicted as a vision of the future given to the seer in the distant past) cast in the form of a conflict between the forces of good and evil. This résumé blends into a description of the divine intervention that is about to transform reality. The transformation takes various forms, from the restoration of paradisaical conditions on this earth to the elevation of the faithful to a higher world (e.g., resurrection, elevation to the stars, assimilation to the heavenly host). Spatial or temporal aspects of the transformation are also emphasized, to a greater or lesser degree. What remains constant, however, is the insistence that humans, no matter what their earthly stature may be, are impotent in influencing either the time or the nature of the outcome. This theme lends the deterministic quality that is characteristic of the apocalyptic writings.

Common Characteristics of Old Testament Apocalyptic Writings

Having set forth a working definition of Old Testament apocalyptic writings, we now fill in the picture by discussing features which, though not belonging to the irreducible nub of those writings, nevertheless do enrich our understanding of the subject.

One of the most important literary contributions of the Jewish apocalyptic seers is the apocalyptic genre. Here the heart of the Old Testament apocalyptic writings, the "vision of a prototypical heavenly order revealed to a religious community through a seer" comes to expression in a distinct literary form. The name "apocalypse" itself comes from the first verse of the New Testament book of Revelation. In fact, the first two verses of that book sketch the basic structure of the genre: "(1) A *revelation* is given by God, (2) through a *mediator* (here Jesus Christ or an angel), (3) to a *seer* concerning (4) *future events.*"[2] This basic structure is found not only in various other parts of the book of Revelation, but also, to give only a few examples, in Daniel 7, 1 Enoch 14–15, 4 Ezra 11–12, and 2 Baruch 53–74. In these apocalypses the seer is granted a glimpse of heavenly events foreshadowing events about to occur on earth that will banish all evil and establish God's reign. Though the presence of many other genres in the apocalyptic writings of the Old Testament and related works does not allow a simple indentification of the apocalyptic genre with Old Testament apocalypses, it is clear that in the formal structure of the apocalypse the message of apocalyptic finds an especially appropriate literary vehicle.

The discussion of the problem of sources of apocalyptic, that is to say, the tradition or traditions out of which the apocalyptic writings developed, has occupied a conspicuous place in scholarship. When the whole corpus of biblical and extra-biblical apocalyptic writings is considered, it becomes evident that one cannot confine the discussion to just one source. That prophetic tradition lies in the background of most apocalyptic writings is clear, and indeed the important connection between biblical prophecy and Jewish apocalyptic can be demonstrated by tracing the unbroken development leading from prophetic eschatology to apocalyptic eschatology.[3] Involved was a gradual shift of emphasis away from this world toward the heavenly world. The eschatology of the prophets was characterized by serious concern for the social, economic, and religious structures and happenings of this world, prompting the prophets to engage in attempts to influence the political leaders of their time and to reform the structures of their nation. By contrast, apocalyptic eschatology tended to maintain weaker connections with the mundane and to emphasize the fallen state of the world and the inevitability of massive judgment and destruction leading to God's creation of a new, righteous order.

It is also clear that many of the apocalyptic writings, especially the so-called pseudepigraphic ones, were influenced by the wisdom tradition. Great delight is exhibited, for example, in lists of cosmological and meteorological phenomena, and with the ordering of various natural realms according to categories.[4] Again, the influence of Persian and Hellenistic traditions and themes has been argued, often with a high degree of plausibility. More important still is the influence of ancient mythological traditions, with the Ugaritic texts of the fourteenth century B.C.E. offering especially striking similarities to many of the mythic motifs appearing in the apocalyptic writings. The influences are therefore diverse (this is especially true of the Old Testament apocalyptic writings), but the most important roots are traceable to biblical prophecy.

Much light has been shed on the social, political, and religious settings of the apocalyptic writings by application of social science methods of research and by comparison with modern apocalyptic phenomena. Apocalyptic is commonly the mode of thought adopted by people who have grown deeply disillusioned with the realities of this world. They feel that the normal channels of power have passed them by. They feel cut off from their own societies, victimized and abandoned. Sociologists have recognized perceptions of deprivation, marginalization, alienation, and disenfranchisement behind both ancient and modern apocalyptic writings. In general, these writings can be interpreted as expressions of protest against prevailing authorities and powers and as products of dissident movements dedicated to supplanting existing structures with radically different ones. As we shall observe in greater detail later, this socio-religious background is important to keep in mind when interpreting the original meaning and theological significance of this literature.

The Apocalyptic Writings in the Old Testament

It is possible to classify the writings within the Old Testament that fit the above definition into three groups. Two of them, which we shall designate the Isaiah and the Zechariah groups, give us examples of early apocalyptic, a transitional stage between prophecy and apocalyptic. In these early apocalyptic writings the central features of full-blown apocalyptic can be seen in an inchoate or emergent form. The third group, consisting of the visions of Daniel 7–12, is the only example found in the Old Testament of full-blown apocalyptic, though Zechariah 12 and 14 come close to that category.

The key to identifying an "Isaiah group" of early apocalyptic writings is found in parts of Isaiah 56–66 (the so-called Third Isaiah), believed to have originated in the period between the Cyrus Edict (which was made public in 538 B.C.E. and enabled the exiled Jews to return to their homeland) and the completion of the second Temple in the year 515 B.C.E. One oracle in Isaiah 65 builds up to a vision of restored Jerusalem, introduced with Yahweh's

> For now, I create new heavens
> and a new earth,
> and the former things will not be remembered,
> nor will they come to mind.
>
> (Isa 65:17, author's trans.)

In dramatic contrast to the adverse conditions described throughout chapters 56–57 and 63–66, conditions under which the faithful suffer oppression and disenfranchisement from their own community, the seer depicts an order in which all sorrow and distress will be removed, and which will supersede the old fallen order as a result of God's creative act. Chapters 57, 59, 65, and 66, however, describe the fallen state of the existing world in shockingly vivid terms. In several passages, especially 59:15*b*-19 and 66:15-16, the intervention of Yahweh is described. Yahweh is depicted as the Divine Warrior who slays all the wicked and delivers the faithful, thus inaugurating the blessed reordering of life described in 65:17-25 (and in other passages, such as 66:10-15).

Isaiah 56–66, taken as a whole, may be classified as early apocalyptic. Since the basic vision of the reordering of reality found in Second Isaiah (Isaiah 40–55 and perhaps 34–35) stands so clearly behind the oracles of Isaiah 56–66, some scholars have convincingly described the latter as the writings of disciples of Second Isaiah and have even designated Second Isaiah as "proto-apocalyptic."

Isaiah 24–27, commonly called the "Isaiah Apocalypse," also belongs to the Isaiah group of early apocalyptic writings. In these chapters the seer portrays the fallen world (e.g., chapter 24) and glimpses the new order that will be inaugurated when God destroys the wicked (symbolized by Moab) and removes sorrow and death from the faithful forever (25:6-12).

Similar visions of the destruction of the old fallen order and the dawn of the new era of blessing are found in Zechariah 12–14 (chapters not attributable to the prophet Zechariah) and Joel 2:28–3:21 (chapters 3–4 in the Hebrew Bible). To a certain degree, Ezekiel 38–39 also belongs to this group, having been added to the sayings of Ezekiel, in my opinion, by a circle that interpreted the prophecy of Ezekiel from an apocalyptic point of view.

The second group of early apocalyptic writings is found in Zechariah 1–6 and stems from the very circle that viewed the Isaiah group as adversarial. These chapters consist primarily of visions received by Zechariah that describe a great reversal, according to which Yahweh will remove all evil and establish in Jerusalem an ideal state for the faithful under the leadership of the High Priest Joshua and Prince Zerubbabel. The point of view of Zechariah is clearly priestly (Zadokite) and grows out of the tradition of the priest-prophet Ezekiel.

Finally, the book of Malachi should be mentioned among works classified as early apocalyptic. Written approximately a half century after Isaiah 56–66 and Zechariah 1–6, it first berates the fallen condition of the community and then announces Yahweh's intervention to purge Judah and Jerusalem of all evil-doers and to re-create a people characterized by perfect obedience. Manifesting a point of view at once priestly and visionary, it likely stems from Levitical priests alienated from what they regard as an apostate cult.[5]

Old Testament apocalyptic reaches its culminating point in chapters 7–12 of Daniel. Coming out of the first major flourish of fully developed Jewish apocalyptic (during which period 1 Enoch 6–36, 85–90, 91:12-17, 93:1-14, and the apocalyptic writings within the sectarian works of Qumran were also produced), Daniel 7–12 portrays the Jewish community afflicted by the anti-Yahwistic campaign of Antiochus IV Epiphanes.[6] Though subjected to terrible persecutions, the people are admonished by the seer, "Daniel," to witness events in heaven that foreshadow a great reversal. The kingdoms of this world would be replaced by the reign of their God, and the people would be vindicated as saints of the Most High, as their enemies were being destroyed. It was primarily through the classic formulation of the apocalyptic vision in Daniel that the noblest and highest apocalyptic themes and symbols of the Old Testament were drawn together so as to become a lasting part of the heritage of both rabbinical Judaism and early Christianity.

The Original Theological Meaning and Significance of the Old Testament Apocalyptic Writings

Once a working definition of Old Testament apocalyptic has been established and the body of writings to be included within this category has been delimited, the next step in interpretation is to establish as accurately as possible the meaning and theological significance of each apocalyptic writing within its original context. This step, accomplished through the application of historical-critical research tools, is a source of controversy in the field of biblical studies in general. Some claim that its aim of reconstructing the historical and social context within which biblical writings arose denies the divine nature of God's Word by drawing attention to human causes. Others argue that such reconstruction both involves excessive subjectivism and occupies the attention of the interpreters to the exclusion of concern with the theological significance of the biblical material.

Some practitioners of historical-critical methods have contributed to the negative image of their approach by building highly speculative theories of origin and by exhibiting a refined disdain for questions of theological meaning or contemporary significance. It is thus very important that care be exercised to avoid highly speculative reconstructions that go beyond the evidence. It is also important that those interested in using up-to-date scientific methods in interpreting the Bible do not become so preoccupied with those methods as to neglect the theological dimensions of the texts. Once these warnings are acknowledged, however, we must state clearly what is at stake in the decision to undertake the difficult task of establishing the meaning of the text in its original context. Properly applied, historical-critical methodology is an honest attempt to allow the texts to confront us with their own messages, rather than reading our views into them (whether consciously or unconsciously).

Historical-critical methodology is not a tool that one may or may not choose to use, depending on one's interests or training. It grows out of the nature of the Bible itself, and the nature of the theology of the Bible. Unlike the writings of mythopoeic cults, which claimed to transmit the timeless truths of the gods in a medium unconnected with the historical experiences of humans, the writings of the Bible, by their own confession, testify to the encounters with God that humans experienced in the happenings of this world. An adequate understanding of ancient Israel's historical recitals, its hymns praising God's acts of deliverance and judgment, and its expressions of hope for the future is simply impossible apart from the disciplined application of historical methods of interpretation suited to shedding light on the original meaning and setting of the biblical writings. To approach such writings as ahistorical truths, detached from specific human experiences, is to betray the historical, incarnational nature of biblical revelation that is one of its unique qualities, when compared with other writings of antiquity.

To be sure, the attempt to establish the original meaning and historical context of the apocalyptic writings involves a greater than average challenge. Writings characterized above all by a visionary mode often offer few clues to their historical context. What is more, the downplaying of the realities of history in favor of heavenly realities leads to a greater detachment from historical happenings than is characteristic of most types of biblical material. Finally, the fact that the apocalyptic seers often utilized an esoteric language comprehensible only to those initiated into their apocalyptic groups adds another obstacle to a historical reading. Such difficulties, however, do not negate the need to establish as clearly as possible the historical setting and meaning of the apocalyptic writings, since no group of writings has been subjected to as much misapplication as those falling under this category. For example, words originally proclaimed to keep the flickering flame of faith alive among those suffering persecution and the loss of all worldly security often have been perverted by modern interpreters into a message extending an invitation to those with influence and power to abdicate social responsibility and bask in visions of otherworldly glory. Thus, by beginning with as clear a notion as possible of the ones to whom the original words were directed and of the circumstances within which that communication occurred, those using the Old Testament for preaching, Bible study, or personal reflection will respect the integrity and autonomy of the biblical text.

The effect on interpretation that such honest reckoning with the original meaning and setting of the apocalyptic writings has will be demonstrated in Part 2, in connection with actual texts. Meanwhile, it is possible to make general observations here. First, it is clear that the apocalyptic writings proclaim a message that rests solidly upon the central confessions of Yahwistic and, especially, prophetic faith. Accordingly, the God of Israel is portrayed as a just and compassionate God who will not forsake the faithful and who will steadfastly guide history according to divine purpose. The apparent victories of those who oppose justice and mercy are therefore not to be taken as definitive, but as trials subsequent to which God will gather those who have suffered for righteousness into a healed and restored creation. Second, it is important to interpret the apocalyptic writings within the context of the Bible as a whole, so that the important lines of connection with other types of biblical literature become apparent and the specific contributions of each section of the Bible become clear. For example, what can at first strike one as bizarre symbolism becomes comprehensible when seen as the vehicle by means of which central tenets of biblical faith are applied to the critical conditions addressed by the seers. The violence and vindictiveness so prominent in many apocalyptic writings are not to be taken as normative expressions of God's presence, but are to be interpreted within the context of a threatening and often chaotic situation. Careful attention to what can be known of the socio-political setting of a given writing thus allows one to appreciate themes of violent conflict and mythological drama which, though hardly suitable for times of normalcy, are fully comprehensible as expressions of the faith of people engulfed by life-threatening crises.

The interpreter approaching an apocalyptic text with an adequate historical-critical method will thus encounter, not a timeless message written for anyone in any setting, but one written for those suffering under specific conditions and struggling to formulate God's word in a manner both continuous with the classical faith of Israel and capable of sustaining a beleaguered community. Upon the basis of such understanding, one concerned with the contemporary significance of a biblical apocalyptic writing can begin the sensitive task of exposition.

III.
THE APPLICABILITY OF APOCALYPTIC TEXTS TO CONTEMPORARY REALITIES

The Problem of Distinguishing Between Reliable and Misleading Interpretations

The historical-critical approach to apocalyptic writings can help in the effort to recover a neglected part of our scriptural heritage. Every person who is dedicated to befriending and ministering to those beset with extreme sorrow, loss, or dislocation will do well to master the art of understanding these probing texts. What is more, every individual and group committed to the cause of justice and peace and to the empowerment of those denied equal rights and opportunities will find their abilities to understand and to act enhanced by the writings of apocalyptic groups, both of biblical times and of our own era. The witness of those who not only suffered persecution but also through faith established their lives on the only foundation that can be shaken by no evil adversary, can deepen the lives of people living in our own troubled times, helping them to establish their lives on the same unshakable foundation. The confession that God is faithful and remains true to righteous purpose, even when everything in the world seems to deny such a belief, becomes a welcomed witness to the one Reality that is dependable in a world as threatening and unreliable as ours.

We thus learn from the apocalyptic writings that the faith expressed in non-apocalyptic sections of Scripture is also authentic as a life source in the inhospitable situations encountered by the friends of mercy and righteousness. Rather than being crushed by adverse experiences, the faithful, according to this model, are preserved as witnesses to and agents of God's righteous reign of peace and justice. By focusing on the ultimate reality of that reign, they are able to experience proleptically the salvation they envision, and thus to endure and to contribute, on behalf of all life, to the healing and restoration of a suffering and battered world. As it would be a great loss to be deprived of the prophetic, hymnic, or sapiential traditions of the Old Testament, so too it would be a loss to be denied the unique contribution that the apocalyptic writings make to our religious heritage.

Though the theological value of the apocalyptic writings should not be overlooked, many thoughtful people today are not very receptive to it because of the apocalyptic messages they hear on television and read in paperback best sellers. If the sensationalism and doomsday dogmatism that characterize much modern interpretation genuinely convey the meaning of the apocalyptic parts of the Bible, such people would either be inclined to dismiss them from their reflection, or would find themselves caught in a deep conflict between their respect for biblical revelation and the natural revulsion they feel toward such a narrow and vindictive outlook on life. This problem raises the necessity of examining examples of popular apocalyptic exposition and prediction.

There is no denying the fact that the mood of the times seems to have created an enormous receptivity to sermons, films, and books devoted to the subject of apocalypticism. Unfortunately, the scriptural reliability of such products seems to have little bearing on their popularity or lack thereof. In fact, the authors and speakers who enjoy the widest audiences are frequently those who show the least respect for the historical meaning of the texts, as they draw the apocalyptic writings into their precise countdown of the world's demise, with vivid descriptions of the accompanying cataclysmic destruction and bloodshed. The appeal of such treatments grows out of the central place occupied in our society by what can be characterized as an "apocalyptic consciousness."[1] Journalists refer to ours as an apocalyptic age, crowds flock to movies with apocalyptic titles and themes, and some political and military leaders confess that they see the arms race between the superpowers leading to a nuclear apocalypse.

It is natural that such a climate should lead to a rekindled interest in bygone ages that similarly felt situated on the edge of the abyss. The figure of Gog of Magog and the destructive fury he unleashed against God's people (Ezekiel 38–39) becomes for many a key to the history of the relations between the United States and the Soviet Union. Daniel's vision of the miraculous eleventh-hour deliverance of the faithful from the end-time woes is translated into the imminent rapture of the elect. The Beast with the seven heads and the Whore of Babylon (of the book of Revelation) are precisely identified with contemporary counterparts and used to describe impending events leading to the glorification of those belonging to the sect in question.

This type of futurism based on the biblical apocalyptic writings has a very old history. Predictions established by numerological calculations have sometimes excited masses of people. Such was the case, for example, in 666 and 1000 C.E. In 1420 in Bohemia, a wandering preacher named Martin Huska attracted a large following through his announcement that the end of the world was to arrive between February 10 and 14. In 1666 a Jewish itinerant named Sabbetai Tzevi attracted a large following in Palestine and other parts of the Near

East after announcing that he was the long-awaited Messiah of Judah. As in the previous cases, the events he announced did not occur, leading to one of the most bizarre endings in the whole history of apocalyptic movements: Sabbetai converted to Islam. Even this did not end the history of apocalyptic enthusiasm. In 1844 the Millerites, a group of Christians in the United States, inspired by a vision of their leader, sold all of their possessions, ascended a mountain, and awaited the return of Christ. These examples indicate that apocalyptic speculations constitute a well-documented part of our spiritual legacy. As indicated by the recent events which one writer called the "apocalypse at Jonestown,"[2] the phenomenon of apocalyptic adventures continues down to the present. The speeches of the Ayatollah Khomeni show that apocalyptic thought is prominent in non-Western cultures as well.

As the year 2000 approaches, we can expect even more use of the Bible in apocalyptic readings of the future, especially if tensions between the superpowers continue and the gap between the wealthy and the poor nations of the world widens. Abetting this development will be accelerated developments in science and technology as well as in life-styles, values, and beliefs. As people face the erosion of traditional values and structures and are torn between a vast array of competing visions of the world and of human purpose, we can expect large numbers to look to the vision of imminent divine intervention to resolve the conflicts they feel and to nurse their feelings of alienation, deprivation, and disenfranchisement. Such people are found not just among the extremely marginalized and down-and-out commonly associated with apocalyptic movements, but in well-established groups as well.

To illustrate this point, let us consider a book that I received in the mail some time ago. I had not ordered it. It simply arrived, bearing the shocking title *Grave and Urgent Warnings from Heaven* and displaying on its cover a picture of a ball of fire descending upon an already ignited earth. Unlike most other unordered mail, this item did not get thrown into the trash. Its subtitle lured me on: *The Communist World Revolution and the Intermediate Coming of the Messiah.* Here was an apocalyptic writing that promised to explain to the reader the meaning of contemporary world affairs and to describe the imminent end of this world and the coming of the messianic age.

The introduction of the book addresses the problem directly:

> As many people know, we are living in apocalyptic times today. So many gigantic problems and frightening evils have arisen in the world, and men have shown such inability or unwillingness to solve

> them, that a great catastrophe for the human race can be the only end result.[3]

The author goes on to promise to explain the future to "the religious man," that is,

> the man of God [who] does not try to drown his mind and heart in the pleasures and obsessions of this passing and dying world [, but who] wishes to know the hard future and to face it. . . . The present work is an attempt to bring the light of divine prophecies to bear upon our present world in order to know its future. We want to understand the details of the coming apocalypse. (p. 3)

As regards the sources from which understanding is to be derived, the author names two vehicles through which the Holy Spirit of God has spoken: "biblical prophecies" and "non-biblical prophecies" (p. 3). The book is especially generous in transmitting the latter, in the form of visions of the future transmitted by various persons, including a woman named Veronica (a housewife from Long Island, New York).

The book's assessment of the condition of the world is bleak: "worldwide famine, epidemics, unabated inflation and unemployment, continual Communist revolutions, and a final nuclear world war now hang over mankind like dark clouds" (p. 7). In no uncertain terms, the end result is described:

"Overwhelming catastrophe is indeed coming to humanity and the Church within the next few years. Unless men heed the Messages from Heaven, over half of humanity will die in a Deluge of fire from above" (p. 11.01). To validate these claims, the author appeals to one of the oracles received by Veronica: "I see a huge Ball! *It's like a Ball of Fire and it's travelling very fast across the sky. Behind it are these streams of fire and rock and . . . I can feel the heat!* Oh! Oh! it's so big—it seems like it's almost on top of us"(p. 11.04).

Who would be motivated to prophesy such doom for the world? And for what reason? These are the kinds of questions the biblical exegete asks of the apocalyptic writings of the Bible as well, and the problems encountered in seeking answers are not dissimilar. In the case of Daniel and the book of Revelation, we know concerning the author only what we can infer from the writings themselves. Though a systematic investigation could possibly lead to the identification of Cyril Marystone (the pseudonymous author of *Grave and Urgent Warnings from Heaven*), we shall content ourselves with the clues offered by the book itself, for this creates a situation similar to the one we face in interpreting the ancient apocalyptic writings of the Bible.

Our first clue is given by Veronica's revelation that the Roman Pontiff is no longer acting as a free agent, but is being held captive by three of the influential advisors of the papacy, namely, Archbishop Giovanni Benelli, Cardinal Jean Vilot, and Archbishop Agostino Casaroli (pp. 11.08-09). The historical and religious setting of this apocalyptic writing thus becomes clear. We have the propaganda of an ultraconservative Catholic person or group that is bitterly opposed to the continuation and extension of the reforms begun by Vatican II. Abandonment of the Latin Mass, adoption of new methods of biblical scholarship, and dialogue with other communities of faith are not taken as signs of progress, but as the work of Satan: "Experimentation, humanism, and modernism are all coming from the deep Pit of Hell" (p. 11.14). Since papal authority cannot be attacked directly without undermining the very appeal to conservative orthodoxy that is the burden of the writing, the blame is placed on the above named advisors, who, though far from strident progressives, nevertheless are too liberal for our protagonist. The changes being introduced by Rome are accordingly not from the pope at all, but from Satan. What are called reforms are actually acts of apostasy and signs of the end time, being part of the overall decline and decay of the world that are leading to the great cataclysm, about to be caused by the Ball of Fire. This apocalyptic writing thus functions as a warning and as a summons to true faith. The reader is admonished to take up the fight against apostate laity, lax priests, and unfaithful leaders of the church, even at the level of the archbishops and leading members of the Curia.

Not only does *Grave and Urgent Warnings* illustrate that apocalyptic writings are still in fashion, even in established circles, but it also gives contemporary expression to several features that lie at the heart of the biblical apocalyptic writings: (1) It is concerned with the renewal of faith and the reordering of life. (2) It bases its message on a vision of heavenly realities. (3) That vision is received in the first instance by a seer (here the prophetess Veronica), who in turn hands it on to the faithful community. (4) Its message unmasks present realities as the works of Satan and draws attention to an awesome divine event that will soon purge away all evil and establish God's true order. (5) The final apocalyptic event will not be the product of human action, nor will human action be able to forestall it, for it will come solely as the result of divine purpose.

Beyond this basic congruence between our working definition of the apocalyptic writings of the Old Testament and *Grave and Urgent Warnings*, we see similarities in other features as well. Veronica's oracles manifest affinities with the biblical genre of the apocalypse. She is shown events in heaven, such as the actions of Michael, Guardian of the Faith. The Queen of Heaven (the Virgin Mary) serves as her interpreter, clarifying the meaning of what she has seen and explaining on the basis of the heavenly events what is about to occur on earth.

The social setting of Marystone's work also bears striking resemblance to the apocalyptic writings of the Bible. Changes within the structures of the church and the world (like the vernacular mass and communist socialism) have led to a sense of marginality, deprivation, alienation, and disenfranchisement for a very conservative group. Though regarding itself as the remnant of true faith, this group feels that it has been removed from centers of power and that it is unable to effect change through the established channels of control. A shocking contradiction is felt between expectations and existing conditions. Whereas economic deprivation is too narrowly understood as one of the factors abetting apocalyptic speculation, this modern example urges a broader definition. Though apocalyptic writings often do arise among the economically impoverished, certain kinds of *relative* deprivation can also serve as a catalyst of apocalyptic feeling, such as a group's sense that its leverage to arrest what are regarded as dangerous trends within church and state has been diminished. It is historically understandable how recourse is thus taken to a vision of heaven, resulting in assurance that the advance of evil will soon be ended by divine intervention, leading to punishment of the wicked and vindication of the righteous. Thus Marystone identifies his own cause with divine purpose and asserts that the apocalyptic promises of the past will find their fulfillment in the grave and urgent events he describes. But is his claim true? Is his message reliable? These are questions that formal similarities to biblical apocalyptic writings in themselves do not answer. To them we shall turn after looking at one further example of contemporary apocalyptic exposition.

In Cyril Marystone's book, biblical sources are distinctly secondary to the revelations of Veronica and other modern seers. Partly for that reason, it is a work that has not been able to command a wide following. Especially among traditionally Bible-oriented readers, such a work can be dismissed as making the Bible subservient to non-biblical sources. Precisely among such readers, however, another apocalyptic writer has become enormously popular, namely Hal Lindsey, who claims to "Tell It Like It Will Be," that is, to give a literal interpretation of what the Bible teaches about the future.[4] Since over ten million people have purchased Lindsey's *Late Great Planet Earth,* and many of them presumably accept his assurances that he is simply explicating what the Bible is saying, we must also look at his approach.

Hal Lindsey reads into the biblical texts his own account of the last days of the world, with total disregard for the historical meaning of these texts.

Far from being an authority for faith, the Bible becomes a lackey at the beck and call of a futurist who apparently harbors a deep death wish for the world and most of its inhabitants. The world will end by 1988 (p. 43). Russia is the Gog described by Ezekiel (pp. 48-60). Egyptian presidents Gamal Abdul Nasser, Anwar Sadat, and Hosni Mubarak have been successively labeled the "king of the South" of Daniel 11:40 (pp. 61-69). The 200 million troops from the East engaging in the battle of Armageddon belong to the People's Republic of China (Rev 9:16; 16:12; 16:16; pp. 70-76). The ten horns of Daniel 7:24 are the nations belonging to the Common Market (pp. 77-76). The harlot of Revelation 17:3-5 is identified with the one church universal to which the ecumenical movement is devoted (pp. 103-23). With careless biblical patchwork, warmed over Scofield Reference Bible dispensationalism, sensationalism, and slick jargon (the rapture is "the ultimate trip"), Lindsey categorically states that he is giving a faithful account of what the Bible says, as he locates the culminating goal of Scripture in a final war ending life as we know it on our planet.

Though Lindsey's book relies heavily on interpretation of biblical texts, and Cyril Marystone's on modern revelations, their basic messages are very similar: Christian faith is depicted as a religion fostering hatred for all humans save those sharing the right interpretation, and embodies a death wish of cosmic proportions. Yet both writers incorporate many of the themes and literary conventions of biblical apocalyptic into their thought, and claim to offer their modern audiences an accurate interpretation of the meaning of the apocalyptic writings of the Bible, a claim accepted by vast numbers of people.

Books like these require us to consider what norms offer reliable guidance in the urgent task of distinguishing between interpretations that are in harmony with biblical faith and those that are misleading. We have already made reference to one such norm, namely, that interpretation of a specific apocalyptic text must relate positively to the message of Scripture as a whole. Against this norm, Hal Lindsey's *Late Great Planet Earth* can be criticized for violating several of the most basic principles of responsible, faithful biblical interpretation: (1) He narrows the focus of interpretation to a limited number of texts taken out of context and read in total disregard of the larger canonical setting. The results of this narrowing include a disdain for the biblical doctrine of creation, a disregard for the compassionate concern for all individuals and nations that unfolds in the Bible, and the sacrifice of the "love commandment," the culminating principle of biblical faith, to a vindictive sectarianism. (2) He treats the historical meaning of the texts with indifference as he exploits them for his apocalyptic system of interpretation. (3) He not only elevates the predictive element of prophecy to a level unjustified by Scripture, but also ties Scripture to a set of speculations that are no more justified than those of Gerald Winrod, Herbert W. Armstrong, or the hundreds of others whose misunderstanding has been exposed by the failure of their predictions to materialize, prior to which they have abetted the cause of hatred, oppression, and war (and often earned millions of dollars doing it). (4) He distorts the lofty moral and spiritual qualities of biblical faith by means of a view of life that demeans both God and humanity. (5) He detracts from the saving and healing power of Scripture through his misinformed and misleading interpretations, and thus confuses rather than enlightens people who look to Scripture for guidance.

Though many other works could be added that illustrate both the fascination with apocalyptic and the abuses commonly perpetrated by its misuse, we have advanced sufficient evidence to establish the need for a method of interpretation that is faithful to Scripture and to the classical values of Judaism and Christianity.

Guidelines for a Faithful Interpretation of Apocalyptic Texts

One of the conclusions we can draw from our criticism of Cyril Marystone and Hal Lindsey is this:

Properly used, the historical-critical method is an indispensible tool in the effort to interpret the apocalyptic writings for contemporary individuals and communities of faith. If interpretation is not anchored in the original meaning of the text, God's Word to our modern situation is lost and is replaced by a highly subjective manipulation of biblical proof-texts.

When applied to the apocalyptic writings of the Old Testament, the historical-critical method has both contextual and historical dimensions. The contextual dimension is concerned with recovering, as completely as the evidence allows, the specific social setting and original meaning of the text being interpreted. All interpretation thus must begin with questions such as, Who is being addressed? By whom? In what setting? And for what reason? To answer these questions is to be concerned with the original Word-event, which in theological terms means the original form of God's address. To posit any other starting point is to lose the objective mooring that alone can place restraints on the ever-present subjective element in interpretation.

Equally important is the historical dimension (canonical context), that is, locating the specific apocalyptic writing within the long history of the covenant relationship between the God of Israel and the people of Israel. Any specific text represents but one moment in that relationship and is not self-contained. Like the moments of any living relationship, a text does not exist in isolation. It draws on earlier moments and points to later ones. Its meaning and significance cannot be determined without this dimension of time and development. Attention to the historical dimension rules out much of the nonsense commonly found in the interpretation of apocalyptic texts. Consider, for example, the common tendency to use the apocalyptic writings to urge the withdrawal of a religious community from involvement in the cause of world peace or social justice, based on the conviction that God will soon destroy this world and most of its inhabitants and snatch the chosen few to heaven. To take these writings within the context of the entire canon means to read them in the light of the central biblical theme of God's care for creation and God's persistent dedication to the rights of all people, especially the neglected rights of the poor and the oppressed. To suspend such biblical concerns in favor of an "ultimate trip" such as that commended by Hal Lindsey—that is, in hallucinations of a "rapture" that will happen no later than 1988 and that will end this world, lifting those with the correct dispensationalist faith out of the conflagration that reduces all others to cinders—is simply unbiblical, not to mention inhumane. By contrast, the God presented by the Bible is a God dedicated to the healing and wholeness of all creation, who calls the faithful into vocations of reconciliation and healing. Ezekiel expresses this central theme of the Bible thus: "As I live, says the Lord God, I have no pleasure in the death of the wicked, but that the wicked turn from his way and live" (33:11*a*; cf. 18:23, 32).

The interpretative approach that is willing to establish the original meaning and canonical context of an apocalyptic writing proceeds from that basis to issues of the contemporary world. That is to say, it does not remain tied to the reconstruction of past events. Though insisting that clarification of the historical meaning and context is an essential starting point, it views the descriptive task as preparatory to an explication of the contemporary meaning and significance of the writings. The goal of this aspect of theological interpretation can be described thus: to assure that these writings mediate God's Word and to awaken modern listeners to God's presence today as they did in biblical times. This means that a given writing cannot become the exclusive vehicle of any individual's or group's private program. It must be viewed as conveying God's Word to the contemporary world. To determine the message inherent in a specimen of biblical apocalyptic written for a specific time and people is one of the most demanding and hazardous aspects of biblical interpretation.

Another way of stating the goal of theological interpretation of biblical texts is this: bringing the essential meaning of those texts to life in corresponding settings today, with corresponding effects. This places historical-critical investigation and contemporary application in very close relation to each other. It means that apocalyptic texts do not say just anything to anyone, but convey specific messages to specific groups. They, like all biblical texts, are dedicated to the restoration of a broken creation to its divinely intended wholeness within a world in which responses to God's redemptive initiatives vary all the way from openness and commitment to hostile opposition.

We shall conclude our general description of apocalyptic writings and their interpretation with an indication of the kinds of messages biblical apocalyptic texts convey to various groups in the world today.

To the oppressed, the deprived, and *the alienated,* the apocalyptic texts disclose an alternative order to the one under which they suffer. It is an order ultimately more real than the present one because it is God's order, the order of the Sovereign One who is revealed above all as the universal agent of compassion and justice. These texts serve to empower such people by relativizing all earthly powers and by confessing that God's order will ultimately prevail. This has the effect of building a firm foundation for faith, and even when the circumstances of life do not permit active social and political engagement, the vision of God's ultimate victory on behalf of the righteous becomes the basis for renewing and preserving hope and integrity and vitality. In the life of shared love, in worship, and in sacrament, the suffering community anticipates the full disclosure of God's reign of peace and justice. This maintains the identity and faith of the community and strengthens it for reengagement in social and political struggles for justice as soon as this becomes humanly possible. Examples from modern history of this function of apocalyptic writings are profoundly inspiring: Hanns Lilje, Martin Niemöller, Dietrich Bonhoeffer, the martyrs of Auschwitz and Dachau, and political prisoners in the Soviet Union, South Africa, and other countries today.

To the oppressors, whether or not they are conscious of obstructing God's order of compassion and justice, the apocalyptic texts give warning of the judgment that will inevitably fall upon those who place personal pettiness, greed, or prejudice in the way of God's order of universal peace. They expose the unreality of all earthly power, the vanity of all worldly projects. They place the oppressor face to face with the ultimate Power who is their Judge and to whom they must account for their actions. They bear witness to the eternal truth, even under circumstances when all else seems to deny it, that ultimately the course of human destiny is determined by moral principles, since that course is guided by the God of justice and compassion. Pictures of judgment and divine wrath within the apocalyptic writings must be understood within the context of this profoundly moral world view; evil will not prevail in the end. To believe otherwise would be to submit to the kind of fatalism that completely undermines the hope and courage that has characterized the lives of the saints throughout our religious history.

To those wavering between dedication to God's order and trust in human ideologies and military-political strategies, the apocalyptic writings come as an admonition: Wake up! Do not be deceived into confusing what the world calls normal or desirable with true value and ultimate standards. Look beyond the circles of the privileged and beneath the prosperity of the elite and discern clearly the fundamental moral struggles occurring both within contemporary societies and across the global community.

When one views the quality of life in modern societies, there are ample reasons for deep concern. Though remarkable prosperity and unprecedented progress in science and technology have characterized the industrial nations of the West and the Far East in the years since World War II, they have been ravaged by very serious problems. Crime, substance abuse, urban blight, racial tension, unemployment, and poverty have persisted and grown more severe. It is difficult to deny that remarkable opportunities have been missed to blend commitment to moral principles with abundant material and technological resources in working toward the amelioration of social decay and the improvement of the quality of our common life. Apathy, ignorance, and an unwillingness to face the hard social and economic facts of our world have played a major role in our dismal record of wide-scale failures. And the economic, legal, and educational structures that we have developed to deal with our problems have been neither sufficiently aggressive nor consistent. In the eyes of millions, the modern, affluent societies of the industrial world are selfish, immoral, and uncaring.

In the streets of these modern societies wander tortured, apocalyptic souls. They have sung songs that have fallen on deaf ears, drawn murals that have been whitewashed, and raised protests that have been swiftly repressed. They have issued warnings of moral disintegration and impending doom. Their leaders and more prosperous fellow citizens have characteristically dismissed their outpourings as deviant and extreme.

We commit a serious error in judgment in refusing to hear the indictments pronounced by the tragic drama of Jonestown, the shocking lyrics of popular songs, and the devastating images of hit videos. The sickness we see has been created not in the first instance by the apocalyptic souls themselves but by the architects and sponsors of heartless and unjust institutions and societies. Though not ignoring the differences between the messages of contemporary apocalyptic outpourings and those of the ancient apocalyptic writings of the Bible, our knowledge of the social conditions fostering apocalyptic enables us to see that apocalyptic should not be dismissed as deviant or irrelevant in any period, for it is the literary manifestation of deep-lying tensions, of social structures that are dangerously out of alignment with acceptable standards and values. In fact, the visions of chaos and impending doom experienced by a society's apocalyptic seers are generally more sensitive to the frailty of life and the forces tearing at the heart of a community than are the projections of more "normal" people. It is an exercise in courage and wisdom to learn to see the world from the vantage point of the apocalypticist, whose visions record not only the inadequacy of our efforts to build a healthy society but also the inevitable complicity of our indifference in the exploitation and injustice that continue to victimize millions of people of all ages.

Though apocalyptic film writers, novelists, and singers may be faulted for heightening our dread of world conflict and nuclear holocaust without contributing toward a reform of harmful attitudes, habits, and practices, they do serve, also on a global scale, to force us to look honestly at the precarious condition of the world in which we live. We may be weary of hearing the anti-nuclear war song "Ninety-nine Red Balloons" and of viewing *The Day After,* but what hope is there for the future if we perfect our propensity for blocking out modern apocalypticists' talk of humanity's destruction of the earth? Though their picture of total destruction must be enveloped within a larger apocalyptic image whose dominant feature is hope, if there is to be a basis for a peaceful and humane future, denial of their terrible litany is an act both of cowardice and of self-deception.

Running parallel to the tragedy of the industrial world's failure to marshal the abundant material and economic resources at its disposal to address the pressing social problems of our time is the tragedy of the great military powers' failure to tame and finally eliminate the unprecedented horror of nuclear war. The options of cowardly denial and courageous affirmative action have been present from the beginning of the nuclear age. In 1959 William Laurence, a reporter who witnessed both the first testing of the atom bomb and the devastation of Hiroshima, wrote a book that cultivated the great deception of the beneficent "nuke" and the magic of human technological ingenuity in keeping always one step ahead of fiery self-destruction. (Is not the latest version of this deception the whole concept of nuclear deterrence through the Strategic Defense Initiative?) With almost spiritual awe, Laurence described this latest of miracles:

> This great iridescent cloud and its mushroom top, I found myself thinking as I watched, is actually a protective umbrella that will forever shield mankind everywhere against the threat of annihilation in any atomic war.
>
> The rising supersun seemed to me the symbol of the dawn of a new era in which any sizable war had become impossible; for no aggressor could start a war without the certainty of absolute and swift annihilation.
>
> This world-covering, protective umbrella, I have since become convinced, will continue shielding us everywhere until the time comes, as come it must, when mankind will be able to beat atomic swords into plowshares, harnessing the vast power of the hydrogen in the world's oceans to bring in an era of prosperity such as the world has never even dared dream about.[5]

Unfortunately, the other voice raised at this fateful threshold of human history, like the proverbial prophetic voice crying in the wilderness, went largely unheeded. It was the wise and sobering voice of Albert Einstein:

> As scientists, . . . we dare not slacken in our efforts to make the peoples of the world, and especially

> their governments, aware of the unspeakable disaster they are certain to provoke unless they change their attitude toward one another and recognize their responsibility in shaping a safe future. . . . The war [World War II] is won, but peace is not. The great powers, united in war, have become divided over peace settlements. The peoples of the world were promised freedom from fear; but the fact is that fear among nations has increased enormously since the end of the war. The world was promised freedom from want; but vast areas of the world face starvation, while elsewhere people live in abundance. The nations of the world were promised liberty and justice; but even now we are witnessing the sad spectacle of armies of "liberation" firing on peoples who demand political independence and social equality. . . . Territorial conflicts and power politics, obsolete as these purposes of national policy may be, still prevail over the essential requirements of human welfare and justice. . . . The prognosis for our postwar world is not bright. The world situation calls for bold action, for a radical change in our approach and our political concepts. Otherwise, our civilization is doomed.[6]

In both the realms of social justice and of world peace, the message of the apocalyptic seer to our generation is urgent. Denial must not be prolonged. We must learn to see the world as it really is, morally weakened and politically in serious disarray. By peering through the eyes of the apocalypticist, we may be instructed in the deeper vision that helps us to see the world as it really is and our involvement in the world as it really is. As we look behind modern apocalypticism to the apocalyptic writings of the ible, we may be open to an even deeper vision, one begetting hope that a system of justice that knows no favorites, a community of compassion that protects the weak, and a peace based on shared prosperity are possible. This is the vision that creates the awareness that peacemakers and advocates of justice struggle not by themselves in the fray. It permits them to recognize at their side the God who frees slaves from their bondage and hears the cries of the oppressed and whose loving power draws all reality toward peace and wholeness.

DO APOCALYPTIC TEXTS SPEAK TO OUR WORLD?

PART TWO

INTRODUCTORY NOTE

In Part 1 we noted that the apocalyptic writings of the Old Testament arose out of crisis situations that demanded a special form of address. The sense of alienation from prevailing social structures, the experience of deprivation, and especially feelings of disillusionment with the fact that the realities of this world appeared to contradict earlier divine promises—these were the social factors abetting apocalyptic responses. Though it is not a literature for all persons in all situations, we have argued that the theological contribution of the apocalyptic writings is considerable, precisely because of the specific situations that they address. We also discovered particular theological themes at the heart of the message of biblical apocalypticism, including an emphasis on the universal scope of divine providence and the relevance of faith at the most troubling points of human existence.

We turn now to illustrate how the message of the

apocalyptic writings can be applied to contemporary realities. As we do so, we shall keep in mind that all such interpretation must be based upon careful attention to the original setting of the texts being considered and to the specific meaning they had within their settings. Only thus can we hope to free the meaning of God's Word from an unbounded subjectivism which would nullify the autonomy of the biblical message. We also stressed that the apocalyptic writings do not stand apart from the central confessions of Scripture, but apply those confessions to particular situations of crisis. The modern interpreter must therefore keep clearly in mind the larger biblical context within which the specific meaning of a given apocalyptic text is to be understood.

In chapter 3 we described in general terms some of the major themes of the apocalyptic writings. The purpose of chapters 4–6 is to focus on actual texts, for only thus can we illustrate how the specific messages of these texts, arising out of their concrete settings, have relevance in relation to contemporary realities. After examining eight examples, we will return to the question of the overall message of Old Testament apocalyptic, for these texts will point beyond themselves to a larger pattern of meaning. We will recognize that pattern as characteristic of biblical apocalyptic and as constituting a unique contribution to biblical theology in the broad sense.

IV.
HUMAN CRISIS

Apocalyptic literature is crisis literature. It arises out of, and addresses humans who are experiencing, the collapse of the structures that previously have upheld the life of the community and the individual. A number of texts in the Old Testament that we can describe as "early apocalyptic" give expression to this sense of collapse and can be seen as the background against which the apocalyptic writings in the Bible developed.

The Collapse of Social Order and the Cry of the Faithful
(Isaiah 59)

Isaiah 59 was composed in Judah in the period shortly after the Edict of Cyrus (538 B.C.E.), which had made it possible for Jewish exiles to return to their homeland. It gives a shocking picture of the situation within which the Jews (both those who had returned from exile and those who had never left the land) found themselves. Included in Isaiah 59 are both a stinging indictment of those who have perverted social and juridical order and a description of Yahweh's anticipated intervention to rectify a deplorable situation. What is the setting of this shocking text?

A clue comes in the master image, appearing in verse 9: "We look for light, and behold, darkness." The contrast between light and darkness runs like a leitmotif through the Isaianic corpus. Both Isaiah of Jerusalem and the prophet of the Exile whom we call Second Isaiah (chapters 40–55) developed this image. In both cases, they did so to give expression to a glorious promise. Though darkness characterized the present situation, Yahweh was about to act to inaugurate a brilliant new era, an era of light:

> The people who walked in darkness
>   have seen a great light;
> those who dwelt in a land of deep darkness,
>   on them has light shined.
>
> (Isa 9:2)

At a time when the land seemed about to be engulfed by internal chaos and foreign invaders, Isaiah looked through the maelstrom of cowardly leaders and threatening armies to the quiet Center, the God of all reality, and from this vantage point announced that light would drive away all darkness.

Isaiah's words of promise and admonition notwithstanding, Judah followed its sister-nation, Israel, along a path of trusting in penultimate powers (what the prophets called false gods), a path that led to the tragedy of the fall of Jerusalem and the destruction of the Temple in 587 B.C.E. Right at the point when the exiled nation was about to lose hope, the image of light and darkness was invoked by the prophet whose words are found in Isaiah 40–55:

> I will turn the darkness before them into light,
> the rough places into level ground.
> (Isa 42:16*b*)

Second Isaiah's message was indeed one of light and promise, and it instilled in the hearts of many the hope to look beyond tragedy to a new era of obedience and blessing as God's people. Again guided by their prophet, they recognized in Cyrus the Persian the agent of Yahweh's deliverance. The Edict of Cyrus was the first step in the dawning of the brilliant light of God's saving act. The next step was the return to the land and the building of a nation modeled after a lofty prophetic vision of a righteous people, a vision again built around the contrast between light and darkness:

> Arise, shine, for your light has come,
> the glory of Yahweh has risen upon you;
> Though darkness covers the earth
> and a deep darkness the peoples,

yet over you Yahweh now rises
and his glory is seen upon you;
Nations will come to your light
and kings to your rising brightness.
(Isa 60:1-3, author's trans.)

Many of the exiles did return. They returned with high expectations of a new era and with an enthusiasm to rebuild Temple and community, fired by prophetic promises. But it was soon apparent that things were not going as expected. The first chapter of the book of Haggai gives a portrait of conditions very much the opposite of what had been expected: Drought, inflation, and fighting between different factions within the Jewish community had led to chaotic conditions that could be described far more adequately in terms of darkness than of light. It is to this situation that Isaiah 59 is also addressed.

Though couched in much symbolism, the portrayal is specific enough to give a vivid picture of the social conditions under which the people were forced to live. Violence and dishonesty had eaten away at the heart of the society until even the law courts could no longer be trusted (vv 3-4). As is typical throughout ages and diverse civilizations, in this situation it was the innocent who fell victim to ruthless opportunists and oppressors (vv 6-8). All that seemed left for the innocent oppressed was to cry up to heaven in the hope that the justice denied them by their earthly leaders would be granted to them by their heavenly Judge:

> Therefore justice is far removed from us,
> and righteousness cannot overtake us.
> We look for light, but all is darkness,
> for brightness, but we walk in gloom.
> (Isa 59:9, author's trans.)

Righteousness and compassion, the foundations upon which the Jewish people were to construct their communal life, had crumbled. The quality of life anticipated by those who had taken up the invitation to return from exile had been perverted:

> Thus justice has turned back
> and righteousness stands far removed,
> for truth has stumbled in the squares
> and uprightness is unable to enter;
> truth is lacking
> and the repentant is robbed.
> (Isa 59:14-15, author's trans.)

The typical prophetic response would have been to address the situation through words and actions aimed at reform of the unjust structures. Thus the prophets of the eighth and seventh centuries delivered scathing indictments, enacted shocking sign acts, and pleaded on behalf of Yahweh for the hearts of the people. While the threat of consequent divine wrath played a part in this appeal for repentance and reform, it was always directed toward the goal of changing social practices and human behavior. In the case of Isaiah 59 and the crisis of the early post-exilic period that produced it, the emphasis has changed. Yahweh's wrath is not threatened as a tactic in bringing a stubborn people to repent. Rather, announcement is made of Yahweh's imminent intervention in human affairs to "even the score" by inflicting stinging punishment on "his adversaries." This climactic section begins with the explicit point that direct divine action was necessitated by a situation in which there was no human instrumentality by which justice could be reestablished. The mode of Yahweh's action is that of the Divine Warrior, that is, the Storm God known in ancient cosmogonic myths from the ancient Sumerian, Babylonian, and Canaanite culture:[1]

> Then Yahweh saw it with his own eyes
> and he realized that there was no justice,
> he saw that there was no man . . .
> was appalled that there was no one to intervene.
> So his own arm brought him victory
> and his righteousness upheld him.
> He put on righteousness as a breastplate,
> the helmet of salvation on his head,
> garments of vengeance as his dress,
> and he wrapped himself in jealousy as a cloak.
> According to deeds he will repay,
> wrath to adversaries, due payment to his enemies,
> to the coastlands he will render requital.

Thus they will fear Yahweh's name from the west,
and his glory from the rising of the sun.
For he will come like a rushing stream
which is driven by the breath of Yahweh.
(Isa 59:15*b*-19, author's trans.)

Isaiah 59 is not an easy chapter for many people to understand. First of all, the gloom expressed in the long lament that leads up to Yahweh's intervention seems to be bleakly pessimistic:

We stumble at noon as if it were dusk,
we smell, though healthy men, like dead men;
We growl like bears, all of us,
and moan continually like doves;
We look for justice, but it does not come,
for salvation, but it is far removed from us.
(Isa 59:10*b*-11, author's trans.)

The manner in which some modern persons formulate their response to this passage is as follows: Is this really the Word of God, or some despairing human word that has found its way into the Bible? Equally troubling for many is the violent behavior attributed to God. Yahweh is literally clothed in the accouterments of war! The offensiveness of such an image of God created difficulty for early Christians, leading Marcion, for example, to distinguish between the wrathful God of the Old Testament and the loving Father of Jesus Christ. This is a "solution" that many Christians still find attractive, as illustrated by this quotation from the German scholar Franz Hesse:

> Manifestly the Old Testament is by no means witness, in the first instance, of the words and actions of *God*. When one opens these books he reads in them about the words and deeds of *Yahweh*, and he reads even more about the very diverse human responses to the words and deeds of Yahweh. . . . 'Yahweh' is by no means solely and exclusively revelation of the living God, but often also mask, disguise.[2]

A solution to the "problem" of the wrath of God as expressed in the Old Testament, by means of surgical excision, contains many theological and social problems. Current perceptions of what constitutes correct behavior would then generate the criteria by which one selects which passages of Scripture are "valid" and by which one constructs one's personal view of God. Scripture thus loses its autonomy, and hence its power to address us from a realm beyond our control.

There is a more profound reason why removal of such passages from our operative canon represents a great loss: We find here addressed aspects of life which, though unpleasant, do not disappear. The god created after our own image of civility and propriety is sufficient for most hours of our privileged existence. But what of the experience of those finding themselves deprived of all human power to control their situation, such as political prisoners, victims of genocide, or those suffering from terminal illnesses? What of those robbed of health, education, and a viable economic status by systemic injustice and social apathy? It is no secret that for those suffering oppression and persecution, such as black slaves in the antebellum United States or Jews and Christians hunted by the Nazis of the Third Reich, a great source of hope and courage was found precisely in apocalyptic texts describing a God who would not tolerate the dominance of injustice and cruelty forever.

Two misconceptions often obstruct our understanding of how those experiencing severe suffering and testing used apocalyptic texts. First, many regard the reappropriation of apocalyptic imagery, such as we find in the black spirituals, as escapist in function. Nothing could be further from the truth. As recent studies have indicated, the imagery of God's intervention and of rewards in heaven did not militate against social activism, but was both the means by which the strength to resist was kept alive and the idiom by which revolutionary strategies were enveloped and promulgated.[3] Second, the application of apocalyptic images of divine intervention is often regarded as representing an inhumane craving for violence based on hatred. But in this case we must be very mindful of the difficulty those enjoying peace and prosperity have in understanding the situation of the oppressed. We must not fail to recognize a central tenet of biblical theology present in the confession of the apocalyptic writers: that even where pernicious and apparently superhuman powers prevail, there is one righteous Power that remains dedicated to the cause of the suffering and the oppressed. Moreover, the vision of God's overthrow of evil culminates in the loftier vision of the new creation in which justice and peace are established and in which the faithful joyfully dedicate themselves to the wholeness of all. Dietrich Bonhoeffer serves as a modern example of the courageous, responsible use of apocalyptic images, for though he was moved by the horrors he experienced during his imprisonment by the Nazis to describe a world severely shaken by the wrath of God and even under the sway of the antichrist, he fully integrated such apocalyptic notions into the central confessions of biblical faith and into a clear definition of the responsible self. This is seen clearly in the following entry in a letter dated 27 November 1943:

> The fact that the horrors of war are now coming home to us with such force will no doubt, if we survive, provide us with the necessary basis for making it possible to reconstruct the life of the

> nations, both spiritually and materially, on Christian principles. So we must try to keep these experiences in our minds, use them in our work, make them bear fruit, and not just shake them off. Never have we been so plainly conscious of the wrath of God, and that is a sign of his grace: "O that today you would hearken to his voice! Harden not your hearts." The tasks that confront us are immense, but we must prepare ourselves for them now and be ready when they come.[4]

Isaiah 59 thus adds a very important element to the biblical message. It is not a word for all people in all situations. It arises out of a crisis within which the order intended by God has collapsed, an order characterized by the presence of a faithful community serving as a life-mediating nucleus in the world, and by God's presence experienced as a source of peace and well-being for all peoples. It is a Word, then, addressed to fallen situations and the victims of such situations, a Word for those denied all human recourse, a Word for those who have been led by their religious leaders to expect great and glorious things of life but who are confronted instead by adversity, tragedy, and persecution. To such people, these parts of Scripture give the assurance that even in the darkest of human situations, God is not absent. In fact, in the worst of all situations, God may be the *only* agent of justice and compassion remaining. Though no one wishes for such tragedy, either for oneself or for any other, should such a time come and should there be only one to intervene, the purest gospel message would surely be this: The One present and eager to save is the God of unfathomable mercy and unbounded power!

The Collapse of the Cult and a Cry for Vindication (Isaiah 66)

The time of crisis in the early post-exilic period brought to the fore another problem, one that had arisen repeatedly during the time of kings and prophets, namely, the role of the cult in the religious life of the people. Frequently, the criticism leveled by the prophets against the Temple and other religious centers has been interpreted as a denial of the legitimacy of religious cults and their sacrificial rites *per se*. This is a misinterpretation. Isaiah can serve as an illustration of this point. Having received his call in the Temple (Isaiah 6), and often drawing the attention of king and people to Zion as Yahweh's chosen place (e.g., Isa 7:1-9; 29:8; 33:20-22), Isaiah clearly looked upon the Temple and its cult as a source of religious vitality. But in the tradition of the earlier prophets (cf. Amos 4:4-5 and 5:18-24), there was one offense that piqued ire more than any other: the use of cultic piety to disguise greed, dishonesty, and an unmerciful heart. Though not as total in his condemnation of the Jerusalem Temple cult as Micah (cf. Mic 3:12), Isaiah was in total agreement with his contemporary that true worship begins with mercy and justice (cf. Mic 6:6-8 with Isa 1:12-17).

The author of Isaiah 66 builds upon this pre-exilic prophetic tradition. As is clear in Isaiah 58, the attack is not on cultic structures or religious customs as such, but on the mixing of formal piety with personal violence and injustice. A further factor complicates the interpretation of Isaiah 66, however. Added to all of the other adversities afflicting the community in Judah in the last four decades of the sixth century B.C.E. was this one: Right at the time when the viability of the community was closely tied to its ability to reconstitute its worship life, rival parties locked in bitter conflict over control of the Temple and the cult. While Haggai, prophetic spokesperson for the Zadokite priesthood, urged a concerted effort to assist Joshua and Zerubbabel in rebuilding the Temple (see Haggai 1), the prophetic group responsible for Isaiah 66 took a position resolutely in opposition to that effort, and identified this opposition with divine will, as we see in the opening two verses:

Yahweh says this:
The heavens are my throne,
and the earth is my footstool.

What is this house which you would build for me,
and what is this throne dais?
All of these things my hand has made,
and all of these things are mine.
But upon this one I will look, the humble,
who is broken in spirit and trembles at my word.
(Isa 66:1-2, author's trans.)

In this case the offended party, excluded from participation in the Temple cult, searches for the center of true faith. It does not locate it in any religious practices as defined and controlled by a human priesthood, but in those qualities of character that define the attitude of the individual toward God: humility, brokenness of spirit, and awe before God's Word. Since there is evidence throughout Isaiah 56–66 that the offended party itself longs for involvement in a righteous cult, we are not dealing with a categorical condemnation of all religious forms. Verse 3 in fact makes clear what is found so objectionable as to evoke Yahweh's wrath: the mixing of cult practices with violence and abominations (the comparative element "like" in most translations is interpretive; the Hebrew text simply juxtaposes the two categories, and then announces the judgment):

Who slaughters an ox and kills a man,
who sacrifices a lamb and breaks a dog's neck,

who presents an offering and (offers) swine's blood,
who burns incense and blesses an idol;
Surely these have chosen their own ways,
they have taken delight in their abomination;
So I in turn will choose hardships for them,
and will bring what they dread upon them.
For I called, but no one would answer,
I spoke but they would not hear;
they did what I consider evil,
what displeases me, that they chose.
(Isa 66: 3-4, author's trans.)

In Part 1 we identified as one of the common experiences leading to an apocalyptic response the sense of disenfranchisement, of being cut off and excluded from the support structures of one's home culture. We encounter just such a sense of disenfranchisement in Isaiah 66. In fact, verse 5 both gives explicit expression to this perception and describes the response growing out of it:

Hear the word of Yahweh,
you who tremble at his word,
Your brethren say, who hate you,
and thrust you out for the sake of my name:
"Let Yahweh display his glory that we may see!"
But I will make you rejoice, while they shall be confounded.
(Isa 66:5, author's trans.)

The word translated "thrust out" can also be translated "excommunicate," which captures a specific connotation that developed in later Hebrew. Ridiculed for its eschatological faith (and in light of the preceding verses, we can assume as well for its opposition to the Zadokite Temple program), the visionary party finds itself excommunicated, cut off from communion within the Temple cult. Where can it turn in hope of vindication? It finds its answer in the very vision that led to its being cut off, namely, the vision of divine vindication! Already introduced by the divine word at the end of the above quoted verse, this theme is developed further in verses 6-16, in which a divine word offers assurance of deliverance and prosperity. We quote only the beginning and end of that passage, since they depict the apocalyptic mode within which the promise of deliverance and vindication is expressed:

> Listen! An uproar from the city,
> a shout from the temple;
> The voice of Yahweh paying in full
> due reward to his enemies.
> . . . .
> For Yahweh is about to come in fire,
> and his chariots will be like the hurricane;
> to pay back his anger in scorching heat,
> and his threat with flames of fire.
> For Yahweh will execute judgment with fire,
> and with his sword against all flesh,
> and those slain by Yahweh will be many.
> (Isa 66:6, 15, author's trans.)

The situation that we can recognize underlying Isaiah 66:1-16 is not a pleasant one. The word it has contributed to the Bible is a harsh one, confounding the attempts of many to understand its theological significance. What are we to make of the picture of Yahweh wielding his sword, executing judgment upon all flesh and slaying many? We must begin, as in all interpretative efforts, by understanding the original situation out of which this passage grew. It is of crucial importance to recognize that it arose out of the most troubling kind of suffering, the kind inflicted by one's own compatriots and religious associates. We are dealing with a period of deep divisions and unprecedented crises within the Jewish community, as an independent-minded people suddenly finds itself both subjugated by a pagan power (Persia) and splintered internally by contending parties. We can lament the fact that the kind of magnanimity expressed just decades earlier by Second Isaiah (e.g., Isa 49:1-6) should have retreated before such a violent and narrow spirit, but it has the effect of shocking us into recognizing that Scripture arose not only out of the sublime moments of human experience, but out of the most troubled ones as well. Given that awareness, one is prepared to recognize the central theme of Isaiah 66, namely, that in all situations God reigns and can be trusted to care for those who cling to God in faith. Again, that confession arises out of situations in which all human experiences seem to deny any basis for hope. It is thus understandable that the mode of the confession is other than gentle magnanimity! The important thing is that the ultimate validity of the standards of righteousness and godliness are upheld and preserved as the only norm that demands the allegiance of the faithful.

It is also essential to remember the second principle of interpretation discussed in Part 1, namely, that this passage should not be interpreted in isolation from the rest of Scripture. It is a particular message to a particular situation, and hence one to be interpreted as only one ingredient in a very rich and diverse biblical heritage. With those limitations clearly in mind, however, we are able to derive both a negative and a positive lesson from Isaiah 66. Negatively, we are able to see that the chaos of inner communal division and conflict can engender a sickness of soul that has a deep effect on a people's vision of God's presence, often abetting the apocalyptic mode with its dualistic tendencies and its violent images. This is the posture of a people whose hopes have dimmed and whose attitudes have grown bitter by experiences of defeat, the loss of a sense of inclusion, and a feeling of powerlessness. Alienated from existing structures, they resort to the vision of direct divine intervention, that is to say, to the apocalyptic vision of ultimate outcome. Positively, we are able to recognize that the faith of the Bible can be embraced under all conditions, even the most adverse and threatening that can be experienced by humans. In Isaiah 66 one of the most astonishing of the confessions of Psalm 139 thus finds vivid expression: "If I make my bed in Sheol, thou art there!" For those facing the specter of total despair and loss of orientation, the example of our ancient biblical ancestors' facing the same grave threat and prevailing through the aid of the apocalyptic vision of God's nearness and power may be nothing less than the most blessed gift under heaven!

Cosmic Collapse and the Longing for Death's Defeat
(Isaiah 24–25)

In chapters 59 and 66 of Isaiah we viewed shocking portraits of the collapse of social order and the disintegration of harmony within the community's religious institutions. In Isaiah 24 and 25 the canvas has been greatly extended. Here we read of the disintegration of the earth itself in an event that brings to the modern mind the specter of nuclear holocaust:

> Behold, the Lord will lay waste the earth
> and make it desolate,
> and he will twist its surface and scatter its inhabitants.
>
> (Isa 24:1)

Clearly the pessimism and despair that we discerned in Isaiah 59 and 66 have deepened even further in this text. We encounter what seems to be an incredible death wish for the entire created order, a virtual reversal of God's first act as recorded in Genesis. Especially since the Bible is frequently cited in support of predictions of the cataclysmic end of the world in our own day, it is important to address the question of how such an apocalyptic portrait in the Bible is to be understood and interpreted.

The problem of reconstructing the original setting and meaning of the text is particularly difficult in the case of chapters 24–27 of Isaiah, a section referred to in scholarly literature as the "Isaiah Apocalypse." Considerations relating both to style and to content point to the late sixth or early fifth century as the time of origin, and to dissident elements within the Jewish community as the protagonists.[5] We seem to be witnessing here the protestations of a group that feels powerless to reform a society that in its eyes has fallen to such a low state of corruption and dissipation as to seal its own doom. Once again the sense of alienation from existing social and cultic structures and of loss of influence and power leads to an apocalyptic posture: What their human efforts are unable to achieve, God will accomplish. Given the total depravity of their generation, that accomplishment would necessitate a terrible judgment on existing realities. The corruption of unrighteousness seems to have permeated all aspects of the world, leading to a dualistic world view within which renewal could occur only after the present order had been brought to an end through judgment and fire.

The major themes of the Isaiah Apocalypse can be seen to arise out of this dualistic world view. We shall describe four of those themes as they are developed in chapters 24 and 25.

First, we find the theme of *social leveling* in 24:2. This is not the yearning of those enjoying positions of power and prestige; in fact, it is not even the position of those whose social status affords them a moderate standard of living. The vision of a time when distinctions between laypersons and priests, between slaves and masters, between customers and merchants, between creditors and debtors, will come to an end is the vision of those experiencing exploitation and oppression under the existing social structures and economic divisions. What is more, it is a vision with a very dignified and ancient history among the Jewish people, a people, after all, born of deliverance from slavery. Part of the purging that is the necessary forerunner to the restoration of justice is thus the elimination of stratification and special privilege that makes it possible for ruthless oppressors to drain the modest possessions and vitality out of the average person. Judgment seen in terms of social leveling was to such people the necessary first step in the re-creation of a just and egalitarian society such as was established by the former slaves after their exodus from Egypt.

The second theme to be developed concerns *the reason for the terrible judgment* that is to befall the earth, and is found in 24:3-6. The source of the calamity is stated expressly at the beginning of this section:

> The earth shall be utterly laid waste and utterly
> despoiled;
> for the Lord has spoken this word.
> (Isa 24:3)

This location of the source of the calamity in the command of Yahweh presses a serious theological problem on the reader, today as in antiquity. What is the nature of the God who commands such a dreadful event as the destruction of the earth? Is this not a capricious act, the act of a wrathful deity recklessly wielding power, unmindful of previous promises and untouched by mercy? The text moves directly to address this serious question:

> The earth mourns and withers,
> the world languishes and withers;
> the heavens languish together with the earth.
> The earth lies polluted
> under its inhabitants;
> for they have transgressed the laws,

violated the statutes,
broken the everlasting covenant.
Therefore a curse devours the earth,
and its inhabitants suffer for their guilt;
therefore the inhabitants of the earth are scorched,
and few men are left.
(Isa 24:4-6)

This section explains the judgment by means of a precise description of its underlying cause (v 5). The calamity is sweeping in its effects: We witness a collapse both of the natural and cosmic world (v 4) and the destruction of the inhabitants of the earth (v 6). At the heart of this calamity lies not the blind wrath and caprice of God, but the blatant repudiation of the covenant by humans. Clearly we are here touching upon a key to this passage, and thus must inquire more deeply into the concept of covenant here being applied.

From earliest times, Israel had developed a profoundly moral concept of reality.[6] At the heart of this concept was the belief that life in harmonious community had been made possible by a gracious act of God, specifically, by God's calling a people forth from life-destructive bondage into life-nurturing community. The essence of this community was the covenant established by God with the delivered people: They were to be obedient to the laws and statutes of the covenant out of gratitude to their God, even as God was to be their protector from all danger. As the Deuteronomist stated it, two paths were placed before Israel: obedience leading to life, and disobedience leading to death (Deut 30:15-20).

This covenantal view, formulated with profundity in the midst of life crises, resulted in a thoroughly consistent understanding of the moral universe within which Israel lived. All threats and difficulties notwithstanding, on the deepest level an abiding harmony was possible for the people that placed God above all other devotions and gratefully accepted the commandments of the covenant as a faithful guide to the blessed life.

The basic concept that human life is situated in a tender balance between life and death has ancient roots antedating even the Hebrew enslavement in Egypt. In the ancient cosmogonic myths of Sumer, Babylon, and Canaan we discern portraits of a world struggling between forces of life and death. Ancient covenant formularies in turn translated this cosmological view into political relationships, promising obedient vassals a life of blessing, while threatening the disobedient with awful curses.

The prophets took this basic view of a moral universe and related it intimately to their understanding of God. The laws and statutes were conceived as having been derived from the heart of a just and loving God and as having been passed on to a chosen people who were to imitate God's ways among humans. They were to be witnesses to the life God intended for all peoples, a life of peace and justice and shared abundance.

Sadly, even tragically, the prophets witnessed a people blessed with this challenge and privilege who were throwing away life's most precious opportunity in favor of false gods and worldly possessions, which ultimately delivered their devotees to death. We see the prophetic response to this tragedy illustrated by Hosea. He boldly portrayed the relation between Yahweh and Israel as the intimate relation between husband and wife (Hosea 1–3). Israel had gone after other lovers to her disgrace and undoing. Rather than abandon her, however, Yahweh continued in the effort of wooing her back (Hosea 11).

Following the marriage metaphor of chapters 1–3, we find a genre specifically addressing the problem of a people forsaking the covenant, the genre of the covenant lawsuit. In the covenant lawsuit found in Hos 4:1-3, Yahweh indicts the people for breaking the covenant, first by pointing to the source of the problem in a total breakdown of the relationship ("there is no faithfulness or kindness, and no knowledge of God in the land"), then by pointing out how all the commandments have been broken like so many falling dominos ("there is swearing, lying, killing, stealing, and committing adultery; they break all bounds and murder follows murder").

When one recalls that the people thus being indicted was the one called by Yahweh to be a source of blessing to all peoples, the tragedy becomes even greater. Not only has a single nation fallen to corruption, but also what was to be a nucleus radiating health and vitality to the whole world is now sowing wrath and judgment instead. The sad result is that the curses accompanying the broken covenant follow, and indeed they move out in ever-growing waves until they encompass all life on the earth:

> Therefore the land mourns,
> and all who dwell on it languish,
> and also the beasts of the field,
> and the birds of the air;
> and even the fish of the sea are taken away.
> (Hos 4:3)

What we see developed here—and Hosea is a true representative of the prophets as a whole—is an utterly moral view of the world and its future.[7] And in this view, Israel, as a carrier of a particular vision of God's nature and will, bears a special responsibility. The future well-being of the world is not an inevitability, but neither are fears of calamity rooted in historical accident or divine caprice. Cosmic harmony is tied to the heart of human community by being the product of a healthy relationship between God and people. For this reason alone, humans can face the future with hope by committing themselves to upholding the covenant in worship and obedience.

What the prophets witnessed, however, was one flagrant breach of covenant after another. It seemed to them that Israel was hell-bent on its own destruction. Isaiah decried the fact that Israel was committed not to the covenant of life, but to a covenant with death (Isa 28:14-15). Jeremiah also despaired over the corruptness of the human heart:

> The heart is deceitful above all things,
> and desperately corrupt;
> who can understand it?
>
> (Jer 17:9)

The corruption that characterized the internal life of the nation was accompanied by growing threats from the major empires of the Near East, giving the later prophets a sense of impending disaster. That disaster struck the Northern Kingdom in 722 B.C.E., resulting in the demise of the Northern Kingdom, Israel. The Southern Kingdom, Judah, succumbed to the blows of the Babylonians in 597 and 587 B.C.E., but even the trials of exile did not seem to teach the people that the only way to peace was through obedience to the covenant. Though the Temple was rebuilt between 520 and 515 B.C.E., it did not secure the quality of obedience for which the prophets had called. One of the last prophetic voices of the Hebrew Bible, found in the book of Malachi, describes the corruption at the heart of the Temple priesthood. What future could there be for such repeat offenders?

Isaiah 24–27 gives expression to the deeper pessimism characteristic of apocalypticism. Not able to abandon the notions of the goodness of God and the faithfulness of God to promises, apocalyptic writers from the late sixth century B.C.E. on down to the common era operated on the premise that faithfulness to the covenant could be restored only by way of a far more thorough-going purging of evil than the one that had occurred in the days of Noah. Indeed, it is out of this conviction that the author of Isaiah 24 explained the impending calamity that he foresaw:

> The earth lies polluted
> under its inhabitants;
> for they have transgressed the laws,
> violated the statutes,
> broken the everlasting covenant.
> (Isa 24:5)

This vision of universal calamity was thus not the product of a blind death wish, but the product of a profoundly tragic, yet consistently moral, view of reality. Given the history of ingratitude and depravity that the post-exilic descendants of the prophets witnessed, an anticipation of continuous peace and prosperity would have been tantamount to the identification of God with an attitude of moral indifference. According to their prophetic view of reality, chronic injustice brings consequences, and if it persists long enough, will have a dreadful impact on all life on the earth.

Despite the pessimistic tone of Isaiah 24–25, the writer is able to peer beyond tragedy with hope. The view developed is actually consistent, for that hope does not rest at all on human potential but is located alone in a transcendent source.

We move with these observations to the third and fourth themes of our text, namely, the themes of *God's presence* and *the defeat of sorrow and death.* The portrait of the collapse of the created order is a frightening one, suggesting a universe reeling out of control, with no one to guide its direction:

> Terror, and the pit, and the snare
>   are upon you, O inhabitant of the earth!
> He who flees at the sound of the terror
>   shall fall into the pit;
> and he who climbs out of the pit
>   shall be caught in the snare.
> For the windows of heaven are opened,
>   and the foundations of the earth tremble.

The earth is utterly broken,
the earth is rent asunder,
the earth is violently shaken.
(Isa 24:17-19)

The image of cosmic collapse par excellence, that of the flood, is invoked to add to the terrifying nature of this passage. As the biblical version of the flood story already brings to mind, such destruction is neither whimsical on the part of the Deity, nor without a purpose that is ultimately redemptive.

The picture of cosmic collapse in Isaiah 24 thus strikes with terror a particular group, namely, the godless. To those suffering for their faith under the tyranny of ruthless oppressors, it is extended as a word of hope, for as the third theme in 24:21-23 indicates, such evil ones do not control the destiny of the world. Ultimately the God of righteousness and compassion is in control and is present to establish the reign of justice and peace through the defeat of all agents of evil, whether in heaven or on the earth:

On that day the Lord will punish
the host of heaven, in heaven,
and the kings of the earth, on the earth.
They will be gathered together
as prisoners in a pit;
they will be shut up in a prison,
and after many days they will be punished.
(Isa 24:21-22)

Though the evil they encounter seems superhuman in stature, the faithful are upheld by the conviction that God has not abandoned them, but is about to act to eliminate all evil powers and to free the earth of their pernicious presence. The end result will be the manifestation of the world's only true Ruler, ending all doubt that those who remain true to God through adversity will ultimately be vindicated and established. This is the purest word of assurance and hope that can be heard by those who remain faithful through persecution and bitter suffering:

> For the Lord of hosts will reign
> on Mount Zion and in Jerusalem
> and before his elders he will manifest his glory.
> (Isa 24:23*b*)

This confession provides the basis for the fourth theme, a theme addressing the hardship and affliction under which the faithful now suffer in a fallen world:

> On this mountain the Lord of hosts will make for all peoples a feast of fat things, a feast of wine on the lees, of fat things full of marrow, of wine on the lees well refined. And he will destroy on this mountain the covering that is cast over all peoples, the veil that is spread over all nations. He will swallow up death for ever, and the Lord God will wipe away tears from all faces, and the reproach of his people he will

> take away from all the earth; for the Lord has spoken. (Isa 25:6-8)

In keeping with the mythological imagery of the Isaiah Apocalypse, which portrays the collapse of the created order as an outcome of the battle of the Divine Warrior and the restoration of order as Yahweh's imprisonment of the host of heaven and the kings of the earth, the theme of the vindication of the faithful is expressed in terms of the banquet that typically celebrated the Divine Warrior's victory. At this banquet, the removal of all that threatened the order of peace and justice intended by God for all creation would be celebrated: the veil of evil's reign, the dark shadow of death, and the sorrow of the oppressed innocent. This restoration of justice and peace thus derives from the same source as the judgment introduced at the beginning of the Isaiah Apocalypse: "for the Lord has spoken" (cf. 24:3*b*).

To this promise of God's reign and the ultimate victory of life over death, there is only one fitting response, namely, a song of praise to the God who does not forget those who remain true to the covenant:

> It will be said on that day, "Lo, this is our God; we have waited for him, that he might save us. This is the Lord; we have waited for him; let us be glad and rejoice in his salvation." (Isa 25:9)

Understood within their original settings and within the context of the larger scriptural heritage, the texts we have studied in this chapter thus constitute a valuable part of our spiritual heritage. In them remarkable courage and the holy imagination of faith come together to assure the afflicted and oppressed of all subsequent ages that while all else may forsake them, God remains true and utterly dependable. In these words, spoken to specific groups within specific situations, we can indeed recognize God's Word, for it is of the essential nature of God's Word in the Bible that it addresses humans in their specificity. It reaches down even to the pits of earthly hell to comfort and to heal. Eschewing every temptation to misuse these texts by offering easy grace to the comfortable and hope to the oppressor, servants of God who are concerned to bring God's Word to those in personal or communal crisis today will apply all the historical knowledge, exegetical skill, and pastoral ability in their possession to proclaiming and interpreting the apocalyptic message so that its relevance is most readily apparent and most deeply appreciated.

V.
BEYOND TRAGEDY: A VISION OF NEW CREATION

Though the texts examined in chapter 4 focused on the theme of collapse, they also pointed beyond human tragedy to divine deliverance. In this chapter we shall look at texts developing the theme of that new beginning lying beyond human tragedy.

The Passing of the Old Order and the Dawn of the New
(Isaiah 34–35)

Isaiah 34–35 seems to constitute a single unit of tradition. Like Isaiah 24–27, these two chapters stem from a period later than the time of the eighth-century prophet under whose name they have been preserved. Scholars have pointed to the close affinity they bear to the themes, vocabulary, and style of Isaiah 40–55, that is, to the so-called Second Isaiah.[1] It is safe to assume that they were written either by that anonymous writer or by a close disciple. While these two chapters do not bear all of the marks of full-blown apocalyptic, they embody one of the central patterns found in the apocalyptic writings of the Bible and therefore can be included here as an early example of the theme of the passing of the old order and the dawn of the new.

Isaiah 34 describes the old order. It begins with an announcement of Yahweh's impending judgment on the nations. The theme of divine wrath against the nations is one of the enigmatic sides of the apocalyptic message that has evoked much theological debate.[2] The issue is particularly vexed by the juxtaposition of magnanimous expressions of divine favor to the nations, found in other parts of Isaiah, such as chapters 19, 42, and 49. How can we explain the sentiments found in chapter 34, such as:

> For the Lord is enraged against all the nations,
> and furious against all their host,
> he has doomed them, has given them over for slaughter.
> Their slain shall be cast out,
> and the stench of their corpses shall rise;
> the mountains shall flow with their blood.
> (Isa 34:2-3)

A clue to this question is found in Isaiah 63:1-6, where Yahweh is portrayed as dripping with the blood of the foreigners who have fallen victim to his holy wrath. What prompted that violent attack was the same motivation we observed in Isaiah 59:

> I looked but there was no helper,
> I was appalled, there was no one to support.
> So my own arm delivered me,
> my wrath supported me.
> I trod down the peoples in my fury,
> I made them drunk in my wrath,
> I poured out their blood on the earth.
> (Isa 63:5-6, author's trans.; cf. 59:16)

In Isaiah 59, the fallen condition of the political and juridical classes in the land had led the dissident visionaries to long for the day when Yahweh would intervene directly to set all things aright. Isaiah 63:1-6 seems to be the corresponding sentiment turned outward against the nations. There too, wickedness seemed to prevail, and agents of righteousness seemed to be totally lacking. The same sickness of soul and desperation that had led to the vision of divine wrath directed at adversaries within the community seems to have led as well to a vision of terrible judgment on all the peoples of the earth. This was not a period of great generosity of soul on the part of the oppressed visionaries. From their point of view, the present order was beyond hope of human reform; both on the national front and the international scene, they could only hope for a direct intervention by the Divine Warrior.[3]

The picture of judgment against the nations takes on cosmic proportions in Isaiah 35:

> All the host of heaven shall rot away,
> and the skies roll up like a scroll.
> All their host shall fall,
> as leaves fall from the vine,
> like leaves falling from the fig tree.
> (Isa 34:5)

Indeed, the entire remaining portion of chapter 34 portrays a creation that has collapsed into chaos, a condition best understood as occasioned by the convulsing of all reality, as the cosmos becomes locked in deadly conflict between the forces of death and life, and Yahweh the Warrior marches forth to destroy Death.

When we move from Isaiah 34 to the next chapter, the change is dramatic:

> The wilderness and the dry land shall be glad,
> the desert shall rejoice and blossom.
> (Isa 35:1)

Thus is introduced the theme of the new creation, the renewal of all reality that can occur once Yahweh has destroyed all who oppose peace and justice. Even as we saw, in the portrait of cosmic collapse in Isaiah 24, that Israel's view of reality was moral through and through, so too we see the same in the picture of new creation in Isaiah 34. Not only is the natural order restored to beauty and vitality, but the whole order of the human community is also reestablished upon the principles of righteousness, compassion, and shared prosperity:

> Strengthen the weak hands,
>   and make firm the feeble knees.
> Say to those who are of a fearful heart,
>   "Be strong, fear not!
> Behold, your God
>   will come with vengeance,
> with the recompense of God.
>   He will come to save you."
> Then the eyes of the blind shall be opened,
>   and the ears of the deaf unstopped;
> then shall the lame man leap like a hart,
>   and the tongue of the dumb sing for joy.
>
> (Isa 35:3-6*a*)

Isaiah 35 thus gives a portrait of a world that is cleansed and healed in all its parts and on all its levels, from the realm of nature to the habitation of humans in society. This vision of renewal culminates in a procession of the faithful as they move to give praise to the gracious God who has restored them and their world to health:

And a highway shall be there,
  and it shall be called the Holy Way,
....
And the ransomed of the Lord shall return,
  and come to Zion with singing;
everlasting joy shall be upon their heads;
  they shall obtain joy and gladness,
  and sorrow and sighing shall flee away.
(Isa 35:8*a*, 10)

New Heavens and the New Earth
(Isaiah 65:17-25)

The vision of God's new creation that we find in Isaiah 65:17-25 is introduced, similarly to Isaiah 59 and 66, by words of harsh indictment and judgment on those who oppress the righteous and pervert the cult by the introduction of pagan practices. True to one of the major themes of biblical apocalyptic, however, the description of the fallen human situation is not the last word. As truly as God reigns, so surely will the fallen order be supplanted by a new creation in which peace and righteousness will be reestablished as the habitation of the faithful.

Once again, it is typical of apocalyptic thought, even in the early form found in Isaiah 65, that a change from a fallen order to a new era of righteousness does not occur through human reform efforts, but through a new, creative act of God:

> For now, I create new heavens
> and a new earth,
> and the former things will not be remembered,
> nor will they come to mind.
> (Isa 65:17, author's trans.)

The qualities of life in the new creation as described in this beautiful vision are again those drawn from the heart of Israel's vision of the righteous, compassionate people of God. This will be a joyous people, one free of weeping and distress. Its inhabitants will live to ripe old age and will enjoy the prosperity of their land. They will be free from the fear of enemy attack, for Yahweh will be in their midst, responding to their prayers. Even the beasts of the field will be drawn into the peace and harmony that will characterize the new order:

> The wolf and the lamb will pasture together,
> the lion will eat straw like the ox,
> and dust will be the serpent's food.
> They will do no harm and no destruction
> in all my holy mountain, says Yahweh.
> (Isa 65:25, author's trans.)

The New Jerusalem
(Zechariah 14)

The vision in Isaiah 65 spoke of Yahweh's creating "Jerusalem a rejoicing." Close to the heart of every visionary was the restoration of the Holy City to a state of holiness and splendor intended solely to glorify God. Zechariah 14 develops this theme in detail.

The chapter begins with Yahweh's announcing a day when he will gather "all the nations" to attack the Holy City, Jerusalem. The devastation of life and property will be terrible. But then there will occur a stunning reversal: "Then Yahweh, my God, will come, and all the holy ones with him" (14:5*b*, author's trans.). The result of Yahweh's intervention will be the inauguration of a totally new era of peace and blessing, which we shall describe shortly.

But first it is important to note that this chapter is building upon a very old tradition and using it to shed light on the ambiguities of the world of many faithful Jews of the early post-exilic era. Though we are unable to establish the provenance of Zechariah 14 with precision, it likely reflects the experience of visionary dissidents of the fifth century B.C.E. They struggled with the twin trials of subjugation under the Persian Empire and the dominance within the Jerusalem cult of a priesthood they deemed defiled and thus responsible for the low state of righteousness and morale in the Jewish community (cf. Malachi 1–2). Their hopes worn thin by repeated setbacks, they no longer felt empowered to initiate reform measures that could reestablish justice and religious freedom in the nation. To keep faith alive, they adopted an apocalyptic outlook and turned to the Divine Warrior for deliverance.[4]

The specific tradition they adopted has deep roots in ancient Near Eastern myth, though it had already been used within the royal theology of the Davidic Dynasty to explain the election and special divine favor enjoyed by the kings of Judah (e.g., Psalm 2). In its original form this myth described the attack of hostile deities on the mountainous habitation of the patron god of a given city-state or empire. The mountain in question was of central importance both for the welfare of the nation and for the stability of the cosmos, for from it the god both reigned over the cosmic hosts and showered prosperity on the earth. An attack on this mountain was thus an attack on the very order and harmony upon which human life depended.[5]

The protagonists of Zechariah felt that the situation within which they lived was just that serious: Adversaries within the community and enemies from foreign lands had formed an ungodly coalition that threatened the very existence of the world. Life was locked in a deadly struggle, most vividly describable in terms of the conflict myth.

The experience of a world permeated with evil not only led to the adoption of this mythic tradition to explain their suffering but also to the shaping of the future hope with which they came to identify themselves. For evil to be defeated and for peace and justice to prevail, nothing less than a new creation was necessary. The form of this new creation would be quite unusual: The polarities at the heart of the old order, such as winter and summer or day and night, would be overcome. There would be continuous light, warmth, and fertility. And the source of this beneficence would be Yahweh's Jerusalem, whence the living waters that fructify the earth would pour forth.

The key to this entire picture of a healed and regenerated creation is found in verse 9: "Then Yahweh will become king over all the earth; on that day Yahweh will be one and his name one" (author's trans.). The fragmentation of the earth that had led to wars between the nations, to bitter conflicts between different parties within the Jewish community, and to the unjust treatment of the weak and the poor could all be traced to a displacement of human devotion. As their hearts turned away from the one true God and became attached to false gods, the harmony of the covenant relationship was ruptured and replaced by chaos in all spheres of life. Fragmentation-begetting chaos could be overcome only in the situation where "Yahweh will be one and his name one." This is perhaps the most fundamental of all religious truths, one grasped and reformulated again and again by the true messengers of God: "Hear, O Israel: The Lord our God is one Lord; and you shall love the Lord your God with all your heart, and with all your soul, and with all your might" (Deut 6:4). Asked to name the commandment that was most important, Jesus quoted this same verse. Saint Augustine added his unforgettable version: "You have made us for yourself, and our hearts are restless until they rest in you" (*Confessions* 1.1). Pointing in the same direction was Paul Tillich's definition of religious faith as "ultimate concern."[6]

Though God's reign was to be universal, as indicated by verses 12-19, there was in Jewish thinking one place on earth where God was present in a special way, and that was in Jerusalem. The transformed earth would make that special status more clear than ever before by nothing less than a geological transformation of the surface of the earth (14:10). The terrible experiences of enemy attack and fiery destruction would be gone forever, the curse removed: "And it shall be inhabited, and never again shall the ban of destruction be upon her; Jerusalem shall be inhabited in safety" (14:11, author's trans.).

Finally, the tensions caused by distinctions between priests and laity, between the sacred and the profane, between the holy and the ordinary, would be overcome in the land. Everywhere God's sovereignty would be acknowledged; all life would become a hymn of praise and an act of sacrifice, and all spheres of existence would find their unity in the God who drew all things into one harmonious whole (14:20-21).

Thus the prayer of the psalm writer would be answered:

> Steadfast love and faithfulness will meet;
>   righteousness and peace will kiss each other.
> Faithfulness will spring up from the ground,
>   and righteousness will look down from the sky.
> Yea, the Lord will give what is good,
>   and our land will yield its increase.
> Righteousness will go before him,
>   and make his footsteps a way.
>
> (Ps 85:10-13)

The picture of a world in which the distinctions that divide individuals from individuals, religions from religions, and nations from nations have been removed and supplanted by unity and harmony, is appealing to many moderns, weary of the torn fabric of society and world. But is not such a view purely utopian? Does it apply in any credible way to our complex and pluralistic world?

There is obviously a serious danger that texts like Isaiah 34–35, Isa 65:17-25, and Zechariah 14 might be used for nationalistic or sectarian purposes to justify the violent repression of persons who differ politically, ideologically, or theologically. Since the earth is to be unified under God's reign and since we are God's people (a religious group might argue), we are entitled to force others to submit to God's purpose by accepting our role in establishing the divine reign.

If the above self-righteous posture is to defer to a faithful one, the two principles of interpretation which we discussed in Part 1 must be kept clearly in mind. First, we must be guided by the original setting out of which these texts arose and to which they were addressed. In doing this, we encounter a suffering and weakened people in no position to inflict its own will upon others. Living under the domination of the Persians and likely stripped of power within its own community, here was a group struggling to preserve the ancestral faith by looking beyond earthly loss to God's reign and to the healing it promised to bring to the earth. Second, when taken within the context of the whole Bible, we recognize that the role of the faithful in relation to God's universal reign of peace and justice does not come to expression in forcing others under one's own political sway but rather in embodying the qualities of God's order through lives of compassion and righteousness dedicated to the healing of *all* creation and to the well-being of *all* people. The vision of God's universal reign, far from becoming a weapon in a particular group's ideological or political warfare, thus becomes the means by which the faithful recognize signs of the new creation, wherever groups are dedicated to the cause of justice and peace and wherever individuals are committed to placing compassion at the center of all their thoughts, actions, and relationships.

VI.
GOD'S REIGN AFFIRMED IN A TIME OF PERSECUTION

The transformation of prophetic eschatology in the direction of a more apocalyptic outlook occurred in the late sixth and early fifth centuries B.C.E. amidst uncertainty vis-à-vis the world situation and under the duress of intracommunity strife. Further transformation into full-blown apocalyptic took place in the first half of the second century B.C.E. during the period when Antiochus IV Epiphanes tried to force Jews to give up exclusive worship of their God and to accept the cosmopolitan cultural and religious beliefs and practices of his program of Hellenization. Within the Hebrew Bible, the last six chapters of the book of Daniel preserve the confessions of Jews refusing to abandon their faith even under the threat of death. We now turn to two samples of this important period in the history of Old Testament apocalyptic.

The Unmasking of This World's Powers by the True Sovereign
(Daniel 7)

How are the faithful to remain true to their confession of the sole sovereignty of God in a world dominated by awesome powers yoked to pagan deities and hostile toward the traditional beliefs and practices of the Jewish people? This question became critical in the early second century B.C.E., as large numbers of Jews betrayed the distinctiveness of their heritage and assimilated into the growing wave of Greek culture.

A courageous and clear answer arose at the most critical point in the confrontation, namely, immediately after the Seleucid king Antiochus IV of Syria desecrated the Temple in Jerusalem by sacrificing a pig upon the altar and erecting in the holy precinct an image of Zeus Olympus (167 B.C.E..). This answer came from the circles of the Hasidim, a group of pious guardians of the faith who placed fidelity to their beliefs above all else and demonstrated their convictions with their very blood. They addressed the crisis in faith by peering beyond the reign of worldly powers to the power of the Sovereign One, whom they believed to be acting true to righteous purposes even when evil seemed to be triumphant. The manner in which they were able to look beyond the apparent realities of this world to the deeper realities of divine purpose was through the apocalyptic vision.

In his vision in chapter 7, Daniel sees four great beasts coming forth out of the sea. These are not normal beasts, as the description of their bizarre appearances indicates. Nor is the sea from which they emerge a normal sea. Both beasts and sea are symbols of primordial chaos, that murky matter that negates all that is good and life-supporting. Drawing from the language of ancient mythic traditions, the seer is able to explain the trials now being experienced by the Jewish community: They are the culmination of a long series of reversals suffered by those faithful to God, beginning with the destruction of Jerusalem by the Babylonians, through the period of Persian domination, and into the era of the Ptolemies and Seleucids, climaxing in the violence of the "horn" of Antiochus IV. Qualitatively, all of these powers were the same: They were agents of chaos, given to violence and destruction.

Over against all their turmoil and rage, the vision catches sight of an austere being of unspeakable dignity and power, "one that was ancient of days." This Glorious One ascends to a throne of judgment, from which he condemns the beasts to destruction (cf. Psalm 82). With one celestial act, the world is cleansed of all agents of evil. In the place of the chaotic beasts, the "Ancient of Days" grants dominion over all nations to "one like a son of man," one whose righteous reign would be everlasting, and thus would secure the faithful ("the people of the saints of the Most High") in a life of peace free of all threats (Dan 7:13, 27).[1]

This remarkable vision gives expression to the audacious faith of a people that looks back on 490 years of subjugation, climaxing in the nightmare of Antiochus IV, and still emerges with a crystal-clear affirmation of the unreality of all earthly imposters. Before the command of the holy God, the nightmare is dispersed, and the reign of the one designated by God becomes the only true reality worthy of the attention of the faithful. It is the assurance that even now this reign is being prepared by God that which gives believers the courage to withstand every trial and to stand firm in their confession that God alone reigns and that the righteous are ultimately secure in God's protection.

As we know from contemporary documents, including 1 and 2 Maccabees, this confession was not a facile one, blissfully ignorant of human tragedy. God's protection did not save the lives of many of the most godly confessors among the Jews, and thus the concept of God's reign had to be enlarged to the point of assimilating the experience of earthly defeat and martyrdom. This development of what aptly has been called "the transcendence of death"[2] (anticipated in Isaiah 25 and announced in Daniel 12, 2 Maccabees, and other writings of the Hellenistic and

Roman periods) is one of the most important contributions made to biblical faith by the apocalyptic vision. Its importance over the centuries in upholding those beset by the most frightening faces of evil, while incalculable, is richly documented in the catacombs of ancient Rome, Nazi prisons and concentration camps, and countless dark places in between and since.

The Posture of the Faithful on the Threshold of a New Age
(Daniel 9)

"O Lord of hosts, how long wilt thou have no mercy on Jerusalem and the cities of Judah, against which thou hast had indignation these seventy years?" This plaintive question, raised heavenward in the year 520 B.C.E. by the prophet Zechariah (Zech 1:12), referred to a divine promise delivered earlier by the prophet Jeremiah that the dominion of foreigners would end after seventy years (Jer 25:12). But instead of seeing signs of imminent restoration, Daniel's community beheld the consolidation of the rule of foreign powers, as well as the unrestored ruins of their Holy City and ubiquitous poverty and despair. "How long. . .?" This truly is one of the questions that abets an apocalyptic outlook. It is also the question that strikes most deeply at the heart of eschatological faith. What is this reality behind earthly realities, for which believers keep waiting? Is it not a mere illusion? Would it not be an act of honesty to accept the harsh realities of this world as the last word and join cause with them?

This critical question arose once again out of the religious crisis of the second century B.C.E. The writer of Daniel 9 looked out over his suffering community, ravaged by Antiochus IV and torn by apostates, and prayed:

> O my God, incline thy ear and hear; open thy eyes and behold our desolations, and the city which is called by thy name; for we do not present our supplications before thee on the ground of our righteousness, but on the ground of thy great mercy. O Lord, hear; O Lord, forgive; O Lord, give heed and act; delay not. (Dan 9:18-19)

To Daniel's prayer, filled with "confessing my sin and the sin of my people Israel" (9:20) and urgent in its appeal for God's intervention, the angel Gabriel brought this response:

> Seventy weeks of years are decreed concerning your people and your holy city, to finish the transgression, to put an end to sin, and to atone for iniquity, to bring in everlasting righteousness, to seal both vision and prophet, and to anoint a most holy place. (9:24)

Clearly the divine promise delivered by Jeremiah in the early sixth century B.C.E. is again being invoked. But with what sleight of hand? Jeremiah promised that seventy years after the Babylonian destruction the subjugation to foreigners would end, making possible the restoration of Jerusalem. But far more than seventy years had passed! Cleverly, a mathematical recalculation is introduced: Not *seventy* years were meant, but *seventy weeks of years,* that is to say, 490 years of desolation were to mark the period from the Babylonian destruction of Jerusalem to the blessed restoration. This put the seer and his audience at the very threshold of the new age. But how satisfying is this answer to the agonizing question, How long?

In Part 1 of this book, we noted how such numbers have been used as the basis for precise calculations of future world events supposedly leading to a final ending of the world as we know it. The fact that Dan 9:24-27 seems to engage in a timetable of its own raises the question of the meaning and significance of such prophecies. There is no denying the fact that numerology played a part in the attempt of ancient apocalyptic communities to puzzle through the enigmas of troubling times. It is also interesting to see that even in the Bible such calculating of a divine timetable led to the necessity of *re*calculations, or to phrase the matter somewhat differently, to the problem of deferred fulfillment. The question concerning the meaning of such biblical calculations is one that can be answered only within the context of the Bible as a whole. Within that context, one sees clearly that plotting exact timetables of end-time events is not a central theme of Scripture. In Gospel tradition, we see Jesus teaching that within the generation of his disciples God's kingdom would draw near (Luke 21:31-32). But he also cautioned against precise predictions and searching for signs of the kingdom's coming; according to Luke 17:21 he announced that the "kingdom of God is in the midst of you."

When approached within the wider context of the Bible, it seems that predictions like the 490 years designated in Daniel 9 function to foster faith and courage in the face of trial and doubt. The significance and meaning of the whole endeavor to determine the time of the final victory of God's order of righteousness and compassion over evil must thus be dealt with within the context of the overall function of the apocalyptic writings: to foster true faith.

The confident announcement of the fulfillment of prophetic promise after seventy years, or seventy weeks of years for that matter, serves the same purpose as the portrayal of the judgment of the beasts emerging from the primordial sea. That purpose is to assure the afflicted that, appearances notwithstanding, there is a righteous, divine order that is more real than any earthly power and that can be trusted utterly and unequivocally. But as the most authentic of all realities, it is not one that can be definitely named, described, or calculated. It is at hand always and in our midst awaiting our acceptance, and yet it is the reality toward which all reality yearns. Either to elevate it exclusively to heavenly realms or to tie it down to the material and predictable is to threaten its essential truth. It is thus wrong to claim that it has validity only in a spiritual sense unrelated to this world, being accessible only to one capable of ecstatic visions. It is also wrong to yoke it to clever predictions and calculations. The reign of God both is and will become, and to preserve this dialectic seers keep inventing metaphors and redoing erroneous calculations, because God's reign always transcends human description and comprehension. Even when carried on in the spirit of humility before the ineffable mystery of divine presence and absence, human miscalculations keep apocalyptic seers humble. This helps to hold their attention to the central message of biblical apocalyptic, namely, that God reigns and is present with all those who in faith face sorrow, tragedy, and persecution courageously and with confidence in the ultimate triumph of righteousness.[3]

Chapters 7 and 9 of Daniel, like the rest of Daniel 7–12 and like the book of Revelation (treated by

Paul S. Minear in a companion volume in this series), remind all who look to the Bible for guidance to be open to the powerful and passionate poetry of those masters of the faith who, even when all hell seemed to engulf them, clung to God as their source of strength and hope, and dared with the imagination of faith to glimpse God's presence even in life's harshest hour. We lose much if we become so unimaginative as to press these writings into a literal reading that exalts the interpreter to a vantage point of clever clairvoyance and condemns humanity and nature to total destruction. We grasp the heart of these writings, however, if in our accepting the divine invitation to become partners with God in the earth's healing we come to treasure our apocalyptic legacy. It is a powerful source of comfort and hope that we can extend to those whose lives totter on the edge of the abyss, and to which we can cling in the time of our own testing.

VII.
CONCLUSION

The diversity of Scripture, when understood properly, represents one of the most dynamic aspects of a unique religious legacy.[1] It points to the fact that biblical revelation is both intrinsically tied to human history and specifically related to individual persons and groups within their particular settings. When care is taken to interpret these writings within their concrete settings, a unique pattern of meaning emerges that constitutes the contribution of the apocalyptic writings to our scriptural heritage. Having considered the specific messages of representative passages in chapters 4–5, we now consider the apocalyptic message as a pattern woven into the fabric of the canon.

One of the recurrent themes of the apocalyptic writings of the Bible is the deadly struggle being waged between the powers of good and evil and the threat thereby posed for all humans. The problems besetting the human race are not viewed in facile terms, as mistakes requiring certain adjustments, but as the culmination of a long history of sinful repudiation of divine will and grace that has brought the world to the brink of total disaster. The world view thus constructed is thoroughly moral and the critique utterly radical. In a hard-hitting manner inherited from the prophets, wicked oppressors, both Jewish and foreign, who pursued their own ambitious schemes at the cost of the suffering of the faithful, the infirm, and the poor, come under the scathing judgment of a holy God. One of the unforgettable lessons of the apocalyptic writings is thus their radical assessment of evil and of the collaboration of humans in the ungodly processes that threatened to destroy the world.

In antiquity this lesson no doubt spoke with a high degree of authority and credibility to those suffering grievously under the powerful oppressors of their time, and perhaps was heard as a warning to many who through complicity or complacency abetted the degradation of human life.

Another of the ubiquitous themes of the biblical apocalyptic writings is the universal reign of the one true God. In a majestic manner, all facets of life and the world are drawn into the drama of the unfolding purpose of the Sovereign God. Though the agents of evil both on earth and in heaven seem to be on the rampage, the visionaries exhibit a remarkable audacity in peering beyond the transitory to the ultimate, which in the mythological symbolism of the time meant peering into the drama of heaven and the conflict of God with the evil hosts. The effect of this peering is the formulation of a clear statement of faith, namely, that God's righteous purpose for reality would prevail and that all of life would finally be drawn into the cosmic harmony of the one true Sovereign.

It is readily apparent how these two themes, radical assessment of evil and daring affirmation of God's sovereignty, constituted the basis for a message of comfort to the faithful in their times of most bitter suffering. We can thus characterize apocalyptic writings as literature that applies the tenets of classical biblical faith to situations of crisis.

We have emphasized earlier how important it is to keep the original message and setting of the apocalyptic writings clearly in mind, in approaching the question of their modern significance. This prevents the co-opting of these writings by those who, whether consciously or unconsciously, are partners in the exploitation of the poor and weak and underprivileged of the earth. In relation to such, a historical reading preserves a harsh word of warning and admonition that dispels false illusions of peace and well-being, through in-depth descriptions of reality, and extends a call to repentance and radical reform. On the other hand, in relation to those denied all earthly sources of hope and comfort the apocalyptic writings (again, historically understood) hold out an uncompromisingly realistic assessment of the human dilemma and a clear confession: God's righteous reign will prevail over all evil, and the faithful will be delivered from all forms of bondage.

Given the very serious problems facing our world, foremost among them global hunger and the nuclear arms race, two themes of apocalyptic literature are conspicuously appropriate: judgment upon oppressors and upon those complacently overlooking systemic structures of injustice, and hope and courage for those finding no earthly source of comfort. The situation we face is serious, but at the same time the divine Power inviting humans to a radical alternative is creatively and redemptively present.

If we remember that the apocalyptic writings are a remarkable ancient example of the courage to look beyond human powerlessness and historical disaster to a new creation willed by God, we can take this part of our scriptural legacy as an invitation to engage our own imaginations, using the idioms and images of our own time, to describe a world reconciled, living in peace and harmony. The radical assessment of evil combined with the vision of God's sovereignty come together in a vision of a global community that gives up tribalism in favor of a commitment to world peace and justice and that realistically sees sacrifice and risk-taking, both on an individual and a national scale, as aspects of thinking beyond war and poverty and hunger. Such modern visions should no more be dismissed as utopian than the visions of the new heavens and new earth of ancient Judaism. Their reality is not measurable alone, or even primarily, in terms of their descriptive accuracy, but above all in terms of their ability to bring the godless to repentance, the oppressed to hope, and the faithful to action. In having these effects, godly visions do have a powerful impact on reality. They destroy obsolete notions and open up human consciousness to righteous alternatives. They break down human barriers and, on the basis of God's universal reign, create the basis for bridge-building that transcends parochial misunderstandings and suspicions. Far from being an exercise in utopian fantasy, such contemporary versions of the apocalyptic vision of a new creation may be the only remaining alternative to another apocalyptic vision whose possibility none of us can deny: the vision of the total destruction of the earth and all who dwell on it.

In our world, a vision of God's alternative to global extinction encounters obstacles, especially in the form of two mental attitudes toward the world situation. One is the attitude of facile optimism and boundless trust in the human (or the national) capacity to meet every challenge and to prevail.

History has demonstrated how tragically misleading such hubris is, yet how seductive it can become, blinding its adherents to illusions of grandeur and invincibility. Against such triumphalism, the apocalyptic legacy projects the foe of every oppressive human institution: the righteous God.

The second destructive attitude is displayed in a guise that makes a far more sympathetic appeal to many. Its adherents begin with a realistic assessment of the human situation that in many ways recalls that of biblical apocalyptic. Then, with grim determination and often with very minimal hopes, they set out to engage in pitched battle with evil and its human agents. Dietrich Bonhoeffer describes the pitfall lying in wait of those espousing this attitude:

> Then there is the man with a *conscience,* who fights single-handedly against heavy odds in situations that call for a decision. But the scale of the conflicts in which he has to choose—with no advice or support except from his own conscience—tears him to pieces.[2]

The way out of the impasse demarcated by facile optimism and grim realism is opened up at the point of confluence between radical critique of evil and radical faith in God's sovereignty, that is to say, at the meeting point of the two fundamental themes of the apocalyptic writings of the Bible. People of faith, both in community and as individuals, can be utterly realistic in their assessment of the human situation and yet not succumb to despair or bitterness, because they act not on the basis of their own programs of reform but as those drawn into God's creative, redemptive purpose on behalf of all humans. People of faith who are drawn into God's purpose are given a dependable basis for transcending the petty schemes and disputes of diverse groups of humans, which seem to be driving the world towards the nightmare of the definitive ending of human history and the extinction of all forms of life on our planet. In the confession that God is present in every struggle for justice and every campaign for peace, empowering all those who accept the reign of righteousness that transcends every claim of special privilege, the faithful today as in ancient times can find a hope-filled path into the future that avoids both heartless arrogance and grim despair, by embracing a vision of a reign of peace and justice uniting all life around one holy Source.

NOTES

I. Why Study the Apocalyptic Writings?

1 Paul Minear, *New Testament Apocalyptic,* Interpreting Biblical Texts, Lloyd R. Bailey and Victor P. Furnish, eds. (Nashville: Abingdon, 1981).

2 Luther did not hold the book of Revelation to be authoritative in the same sense as most other biblical books, referring to it, for example, as "hardly of such significance as to be useful for citing in controversy" (*Luther's Works,* vol. 36, A. R. Wentz and H. T. Lehmann, eds. [Philadelphia: Muhlenberg, 1959] 140). D. H. Lawrence offered this biting critique (*Apocalypse* [New York: Viking, 1932] 20-21):

> The Apocalypse of John is, as it stands, the work of a second-rate mind. It appeals intensely to second-rate minds in every country and every century. Strangely enough, unintelligible as it is, it has no doubt been the greatest source of inspiration of the vast mass of Christian minds—the vast mass being always second rate—since the first century, and we realize, to our horror, that this is what we are up against today; not Jesus nor Paul, but John of Patmos.

3 Foremost among the proponents of this system of interpretation is Hal Lindsey (*Late Great Planet Earth* [Grand Rapids, Mich.: Zondervan, 1970]). Cf. William Martin, "Waiting for the End," *The Atlantic Monthly* (June 1982) 31-37; Roy Harrisville, "Tomorrow with Hal Lindsey," *Dialog* 3 (1974) 290-96. See also Robert Scheer, *With Enough Shovels: Reagan, Bush and Nuclear War* (New York: Random House, 1982); Jonathan Schell, *The Fate of the Earth* (New York: Avon, 1982).

4 *The Bhagavad Gita* (New York: Penguin Books, 1962). These descriptions of Krishna from the *Bhagavad Gita* were recalled by J. Robert Oppenheimer, chief architect of the atom bomb, as he witnessed the first successful nuclear explosion at the Trinity test site in New Mexico (Richard Rhodes, " 'I Am Become Death. . . ' The Agony of J. Robert Oppenheimer," *American Heritage* 28, no. 6 (Oct. 1977) 70-78.

5 Carl G. Jung, *Man and His Symbols* (New York: Dell, 1968) 75.

6 Paul D. Hanson, "The Apocalyptic Consciousness," *Quarterly Review* 4 (1984) 23–39.

II. Defining Old Testament Apocalyptic

1 See J. Block, *On the Apocalyptic in Judaism,* JQRMS 2 (Philadelphia: Dropsie College, 1952).

2 Paul D. Hanson, "Apocalypse, Genre," in *IDB Sup,* Keith Crim et al., eds. (Nashville: Abingdon, 1976) 27.

3 For a discussion of the relation between prophetic eschatology and apocalyptic eschatology, see Paul D. Hanson, *The Dawn of Apocalyptic,* 2nd ed. (Philadelphia: Fortress, 1979) 7-12.

4 See Michael Stone, "Lists of Revealed Things in Apocalyptic Literature," in *Magnalia Dei: The Mighty Acts of God, Essays on the Bible and Archaeology in Memory of G. Ernest Wright,* F. M. Cross, W. E. Lemke, and P. D. Miller, Jr., eds. (Garden City, N.Y.: Doubleday, 1976) 414-52.

5 See Paul D. Hanson, *The People Called: The Growth of Community in the Bible* (San Francisco: Harper & Row, 1986).

6 See John J. Collins, *The Apocalyptic Vision of the Book of Daniel,* HSM 16 (Missoula, Mont.: Scholars, 1977) 191-222.

III. The Applicability of Apocalyptic Texts to Contemporary Realities

1 See Paul D. Hanson, "Apocalyptic Consciousness," *Quarterly Review* 4 (1984) 23-39.

2 John R. Hall, "Apocalypse at Jonestown," *Transaction* (September/October 1979) 55-62.
3 Cyril Marystone, *Grave and Urgent Warnings from Heaven: The Communist World Revolution and the Intermediate Coming of the Messiah* (no copyright) 3. Subsequent page references in text.
4 Hal Lindsey, *The Late Great Planet Earth* (Grand Rapids, Mich.: Zondervan, 1970) 7. Subsequent page references in text.
5 William L. Laurence, *Men and Atoms: The Story of the Atomic Bomb* (New York: Alfred A. Knopf, 1946) 197.
6 Otto Nathan and Heinz Norden, eds., *Einstein on Peace* (New York: Harper & Row, 1980) 355-56.

IV. Human Crisis

1 See Patrick D. Miller, Jr., *The Divine Warrior in Early Israel,* HSM 5 (Cambridge, Mass.: Harvard, 1973).
2 Franz Hesse, "The Evaluation and the Authority of Old Testament Texts," in *Essays on Old Testament Hermeneutics,* Claus Westermann, ed. (Richmond, Va.: John Knox, 1963) 299.
3 See James H. Cone, *The Spirituals and the Blues* (New York: Seabury, 1972).
4 Dietrich Bonhoeffer, *Letters and Papers from Prison*, Eberhard Bethge, ed. (New York: Macmillan, 1971) 146.
5 See William R. Millar, *Isaiah 24–27 and the Origin of Apocalyptic,* HSM 11(Missoula, Mont.: Scholars, 1976).
6 For a fuller description of ancient Israel's ethical view of the world, see Paul D. Hanson, *The People Called: The Growth of Community in the Bible* (San Francisco: Harper & Row, 1986).
7 Ibid., 158-67.

V. Beyond Tragedy: A Vision of New Creation

1 See Marvin Pope, "Isaiah xxxiv in Relation to Isaiah xxxv, xl-lxvi," *JBL* 71 (1952) 235-43.

2 See Paul D. Hanson, "War and Peace in the Hebrew Bible," *Interpretation* 38 (1984) 341-62.
3 See Paul D. Hanson, *The Dawn of Apocalyptic* (Philadelphia: Fortress, 1979) 203-8.
4 Ibid., 369-80.
5 See Richard J. Clifford, S.J., *The Cosmic Mountain in Canaan and the Old Testament* (Cambridge, Mass.: Harvard, 1972).
6 Paul Tillich, *Systematic Theology,* vol. 1 (Chicago: University of Chicago, 1951) 11-15, 155-57.

VI. God's Reign Affirmed in a Time of Persecution

1 See John J. Collins, *The Apocalyptic Vision of the Book of Daniel,* HSM 16 (Missoula, Mont.: Scholars, 1977) 123-47.
2 John J. Collins, "Jewish Apocalyptic as the Transcendence of Death," *CBQ* 36 (1974) 21-43.
3 See Paul D. Hanson, *The Diversity of Scripture* (Philadelphia: Fortress, 1982) 37-62.

VII. Conclusion

1 See Paul D. Hanson, *The Diversity of Scripture* (Philadelphia: Fortress, 1982).
2 Dietrich Bonhoeffer, *Letters and Papers from Prison,* Eberhard Bethge, ed. (New York: Macmillan, 1971) 4.

AIDS FOR THE INTERPRETER

General Works

The reader may want to use the translation of the Bible that is quoted most extensively in this study, the Revised Standard Version (available in a very useful annotated edition, *The New Oxford Annotated Bible with the Apocrypha,* 1973). Comparison between translations is often helpful, and for this purpose the following versions are recommended: *The New Jerusalem Bible,* the Jewish Publication Society Bible (*The Torah, The Prophets,* and *The Writings*), and *The New English Bible.*

For general reference, the following are helpful and reliable: *The Interpreter's Dictionary of the Bible,* 5 vols. (Nashville: Abingdon, 1962, 1976), and *Harper's Bible Dictionary* (San Francisco: Harper & Row, 1985).

Old Testament Apocalyptic

For a general orientation to the apocalyptic literature of the Bible, one could read "An Overview of Early Jewish and Christian Apocalypticism," found on pages 427-44 of the 1979 edition of my book, *The Dawn of Apocalyptic* (Philadelphia: Fortress). A fine recent book treating the apocalyptic writings of the Hellenistic and Roman periods is John J. Collins, *The Apocalyptic Imagination: An Introduction to the Jewish Matrix of Christianity* (New York: Crossroad, 1984).

The search for the socio-historical context of the earliest apocalyptic writings in the Bible focuses on the transition from late prophecy to apocalyptic and on additions that were made to some of the prophetic books during that period of transition. For Isaiah 24–27 (the so-called "Isaiah Apocalypse"), William R. Millar's study is helpful: *Isaiah 24–27 and the Origin of Apocalyptic,* HSM 11(Missoula, Mont.: Scholar Press, 1976). For Isaiah 56–66 and Zechariah 9–14, the reader is referred to my study, *The Dawn of Apocalyptic,* and David L. Petersen's *Late Israelite Prophecy: Studies in Deutero-Prophetic Literature and in Chronicles* (Society of Biblical Literature Monograph Series 23 [Missoula, Mont.: Scholar Press, 1977]).

The book of Daniel obviously enjoys a preeminent position among the Old Testament apocalyptic writings, for in chapters 7–12 of that book apocalyptic thought reaches a mature stage. Within the vast literature on the book of Daniel, the following are of special interest: W. S. Towner, *Daniel* (Atlanta: John Knox, 1984); A. Lacocque, *The Book of Daniel* (Atlanta: John Knox, 1979); Lewis F. Hartman and Alexander A. DiLella, *Daniel* (AB 23 [New York: Doubleday, 1978]); and J. J. Collins, *The Apocalyptic Vision of the Book of Daniel* (HSM 16 [Missoula, Mont.: Scholar Press, 1977]).

For the one lured to apocalyptic works beyond the Bible, the pseudepigraphic writings of this type are found in new translations in *The Old Testament Pseudepigrapha,* vol. 1, James H. Charlesworth, ed. (Garden City, N.Y.: Doubleday, 1984). A valuable guide to these often bewildering writings is provided by George W. E.

Nickelsburg, *Jewish Literature Between the Bible and the Mishnah* (Philadelphia: Fortress, 1981).

The theological interpretation and contemporary application of the apocalyptic writings has a long history, much of which unfortunately has not influenced current popular writers on this topic. Among older works, the one whose value has endured more than any other is perhaps H. H. Rowley's *The Relevance of Apocalyptic* (New York: Association, 1963). See also the thorough study of D. S. Russell, *The Method and Message of Jewish Apocalyptic* (Philadelphia: Westminster, 1964). Klaus Koch reopens the issue of the meaning of apocalyptic in his book, *The Rediscovery of Apocalyptic* (SBT 22 [London: SCM, 1972]). See also the introduction and the essays gathered in Paul D. Hanson, ed., *Visionaries and Their Apocalypses* (Issues in Religion and Theology 4 [Philadelphia: Fortress, 1983]), and chapter 3, "Apocalyptic Seers and Priests in Conflict, and the Development of the Visionary/Pragmatic Polarity" in my book, *The Diversity of Scripture: A Theological Interpretation* (Overtures to Biblical Theology 11 [Philadelphia: Fortress, 1982]), as well as chapters 7–12 in my book, *The People Called: The Growth of Community in the Bible* (San Francisco: Harper & Row, 1986).

Concerning the lively debate over apocalypticism among systematic theologians, the reader will find helpful Carl E. Braaten's book, *Christ and Counter-Christ: Apocalyptic Themes in Theology and Culture* (Philadelphia: Fortress, 1972).